zero²
success

10 KEYS TO CREATING A VERY PROFITABLE BUSINESS
BY _LEGALLY_ KEEPING MORE OF WHAT YOU MAKE!

Andrew Miles, J.D.
America's Top Tax Strategist
and Asset Protection Expert

Morgan James Publishing • New York

Zero To Success

10 Keys To Creating A Very Profitable Business
By _Legally_ Keeping More Of What You Make

Copyright © 2006
Pathfinder Business Strategies, LLC
All rights reserved.

ISBN: 1-60037-166-3 (Paperback)

ISBN: 1-60037-167-1 (Hardcover)

ISBN: 1-60037-168-X (eBook)

MORGAN · JAMES
THE ENTREPRENEURIAL PUBLISHER ™
www.morganjamespublishing.com

Morgan James Publishing, LLC
1225 Franklin Ave., Ste. 325
Garden City, NY 11530-1693
Toll Free 800-485-4943
www.MorganJamesPublishing.com

Habitat for Humanity®
Peninsula
Building Partner

Cover Design by:
Rob Davis
rdavis@meshnyc.com

Interior Design by:
Kimberly Lydon Stevenson
kim@spotcolordesign.com

about the author

Drew Miles

After growing up in a family business, Drew went on to graduate college in a 3 year accelerated program with honors; cum laude and a member of the Phi Beta Kappa academic fraternity. He is trained as an attorney and practiced in the State of New York for 12 years as the senior partner of his own firm specializing in the areas of business and real estate. He is a member of both the State and Federal Bars.

Drew is a successful real estate investor and businessman, having started and developed numerous businesses. However, dissatisfied with his own financial progress, he enrolled himself in a rigorous five year financial education. During this "informal education" he was trained by such people as Robert (Rich Dad-Poor Dad) Kiyosaki, Ted Thomas, John Burley, Anthony Robbins, Dr. Van Tharp, Al (C.W.) Allen, Dr. Donald Moine.

Drew has combined all that he learned during his formal education, 'informal' education and twenty-five years of business experience in the development of programs designed that teach people how to build and preserve lasting wealth. He is an author, teacher and international speaker in the areas of wealth building, asset protection and tax saving strategies.

He has benefited from the strategies he teaches and helped his students save thousands and thousands of dollars in the process. That's why he's nationally known as *The Wealth Building Attorney*.

acknowledgements

Like building wealth, writing a book is a team effort, and I'd like to take a moment to thank my team.

My wife Mari has provided me with a new sense of purpose and motivation. It would be hardly worth waking up without her by my side.

I've had many teachers and mentors over the years that helped me grow from a disenchanted attorney into a prospering businessman. Robert Kiyosaki, Ted Thomas, Mike Litman, Al (C.W.) Allen, John Burley and my many coaches and others who provided inspiration and guidance along the way. I thank you all.

Heartfelt thanks go to Herman Bader and Georgann Fuller who gave me a helping hand up when I really needed it.

I thank my family, friends and staff at the "Pathfinder Family" offices who have all given me a great deal of support.

To Jim Sullivan who lit the spark in a rental car outside the Center Moriches diner. Who woulda thunk? ..... And to my Lord and Savior Jesus Christ who came into my life in a new way that day and, as a result, everything has been made new.

testimonials

Praise for Zero 2 Success

"In this fascinating new book, *Zero 2 Success*, attorney and success coach Drew Miles shares dozens of powerful strategies for both reducing taxes and gaining protection from legal liability. Written in an inspirational style, this is a unique book that will literally save some readers tens of thousands of dollars."

Donald Moine, Ph.D.
Author & International Business Consultant

"Financial Freedom doesn't come by accident. Drew Miles has taught thousands of people all over the U.S. and Canada how to get from where they are financially to where they want to go. He can do the same thing for you."

Jason Oman
#1 Best Selling Author of
Conversations with Millionaires* & *Money On Demand

"Drew Miles is dedicated to helping people create wealth. If you would like more financial success in your life this book is a must read."

Eric Lofholm
President, Eric Lofholm International, Inc.

"Drew Miles teaches people how to become wealthy and stay that way. Whether you're a fledgling entrepreneur or a seasoned business veteran, you MUST listen to his advice and give yourself a much deserved raise from Uncle Sam."

Matt Bacak
The Powerful Promoter

foreword

Congratulations on investing in this book! If you take action on what you read here, you will have an excellent vehicle to drive you toward your goals and dreams. And since Drew uses driving as a metaphor, I will too. So what you need to do right now is get ready to put the pedal to the metal, because this book is your race car for the road to success.

Drew Miles makes some important points in this book. No journey is complete without a little "packing" to prepare you for the trip. The first chapter helps you understand the importance of having a business instead of working for someone else as an employee. Owning your own business is the only way to get ahead financially. When you're working for someone else, your boss is the one getting rich because of your efforts. Not you.

What else do you need for a journey? A guide, of course. The second chapter will exhort you to find mentors and coaches who will serve as your Global Positioning System—your GPS for success. They will help you cut way down on your learning curve and avoid road hazards. If you learn nothing else from this book, I hope you will come away with an understanding of how critical it is for you to hire excellent coaches and mentors. You absolutely cannot succeed in business without them.

The next several chapters will help you create the right structure for your business, choose the kind of business you want to run, and begin to promote yourself. Case studies will help you understand how different businesses work. This will help you decide what kind of company makes the best use of your skills and resources.

The chapters after that give some excellent guidance on bookkeeping and financial management, putting systems in place that keep your business humming like a well maintained car: goal setting, time management and written agreements. You'll also discover how to leverage relationships to power your business.

Have you ever gotten in your car and just started driving aimlessly? Maybe once or twice for a pleasant Sunday outing, but you would never leave your home every day with no clue where you were going, right? Before you begin your own journey from zero to success, you must have a "road map." Chapter 9 empowers you to create your own simple but effective business plan that will help keep you on track.

This is where the rubber meets the road. This is where you make one of the most important decisions of your life. So get in the driver's seat and be ready to win the checkered flag.

Glenn Dietzel
Awakened, LLC
http://www.AwakenTheAuthorWithin.com

introduction

Ten years ago, when I decided to take my business life to a new level, there weren't all that many resources. Many of the books that had been written were more inspirational than instructional, good business seminars were few and far between. Coaching was just starting to catch on and mentors weren't yet in vogue.

As a result, I had to work VERY hard to break out of the mold I had created for myself.

In a few short years I read over 500 books, listened and re-listened to thousands of hours of tapes and moved forward mostly by trial and error. It seemed like my progress could be measured by 'one step forward and two steps back'. But I persisted. In fact, looking back, my persistence was my biggest asset.

As my abilities grew, I often repeated to myself "someone ought to write a book, a manual, a how-to guide, yes, a *blueprint*, for properly identifying, launching and growing a successful business. It would save folks a lot of time, energy, money and pain".

This book is that blueprint.

Inside these pages, you'll learn how to select the right business and set it up in the proper entity. You'll learn how to systematize it so it runs smoothly and how to maximize the tax benefits—which are incredible. You'll learn how to protect your assets and market your business successfully. And you'll learn to manage yourself and your time, so you still have an opportunity to live the rest of your life.

A mentor once shared these words of wisdom and now I pass the torch on to you:

"Don't ask yourself what the world needs. Ask yourself what makes you come alive, and go do that, because what the world needs is people who have come alive."

You can make a fortune doing virtually anything. Choose something that makes you come alive.

Drew Miles
Vero Beach, Florida
July 2005

Table of Contents

Congratulations! You're ready for your Next Step.

Why Have Your Own Business?

Those who start out with too little money
are more likely to succeed
than those who start out with too much.
Energy and imagination are the springboards
to wealth creation.
-Brian Tracy

There is only one reason to have a business—to get ahead financially.

The purpose of business is to **generate a profit**, plain and simple. It's not that it can't be exciting, but that's not the main purpose of building a business. It's not that it can't be a creative endeavor—it can, but that's not the primary purpose. And it's not that it can't provide freedom and fulfillment. All of these things can be a reality for any business, but they are not the main reason for putting your time and energy into building a business.

Again, the main reason for having a business is to get ahead financially.

For those of you who grew up in the "E" quadrant (1) surrounded by friends and family members who are employees, the idea of having your own business probably sounds foreign, even risky. I'm willing to bet that your loved ones will discourage you from starting your own business. After all, wasn't it your parents who said "Go to school, get good grades and find a good, secure job"? And your friend's parents taught them the same thing.

I'll never forget my first real estate investment. I was in my first year of law school and I decided to buy a house and rent it out. I finished the lower level and made a duplex out of it in order to double the rental income. One of my friends offered to help me out on weekends, and after about six weekends of hard work, the lower unit was ready for a tenant.

During those weekends, we'd talk a lot about real estate and investing, and he began to "get the bug". He realized that it was a step by step process and that if you followed a certain formula you'd achieve the desired result. We began to discuss doing a deal together.

Somewhere along the way, he must have shared his new ideas with his family because one weekend he told me he could not do the deal we were contemplating. When I asked him why, he said, "Because my father said the sewer could back up and I'd have a real problem on my hands".

I was dumbfounded! "You mean to tell me that a problem like that would scare you away from the benefits of investing? Tell me you don't have the money. Tell me you don't know anything about real estate. Tell me you're just plain afraid. I can understand that, but the sewer?"

He agreed with me, but then he said his father asked him the question, "What would you do if the sewer backed up?", and that got him thinking about the risks involved. So I said, forgive me for being rude, but I'd just call a plumber and let him fix it. It just didn't seem to be that big a problem to me.

Later, I realized that his concern had much less to do with the plumbing than with the whole idea of business and investing. You see, his father had worked for the same company, in the textile business for twenty-five years. He had a decent salary, good benefits and two weeks off each year to vacation with his family. That was his financial reality and, to him, my idea seemed crazy, perhaps even a little reckless.

Two years later I sold that property for a profit of almost $30,000. Of course, I had my share of obstacles along the way, but so do employees. No one is immune to having challenges in life. Yet, if you want to get ahead financially, you have to accept challenges that can lead you to your financial freedom instead of the boss's financial freedom. Once you've made that decision, it's a matter of surrounding yourself with great coaches and mentors and learning to work through the problems one by one. Chapter two looks at mentors and coaches.

No doubt, many thousands of businesses fail each year. That's no reason to shy away. The ground rules are different for having a business and, once you learn them, you can enjoy all of the benefits that come with operating your own business.

What IS a Business?

A business is any endeavor that we engage in for the purpose of making a profit. It doesn't matter what the subject of the business is. It can be a service company; it can create and sell products; it can be information based; or it can involve the use of equipment such as computers or manufacturing machines. Later in this book, I'll outline some of the thousands and thousands of businesses you can choose from.

For our purpose right now, the thing that distinguishes a business from every other kind of activity is the intention to make a profit. This is HUGELY important.

What a Business IS NOT.

I'm stressing this point because many people confuse their method of self-expression with business.

For example, a business should not be viewed as a way to spend time doing what you like. That's a hobby or a passion or a calling. It's not a business. Don't get me wrong. The subject of your business can and should be something you're passionate about (I love teaching people how to build and protect wealth), but it is easy to confuse your hobby and your business and that confusion can be financially devastating.

Your business should be fun, but that's not its main purpose. It should give you freedom, but that's not its first goal.

Your business can be one of the most rewarding, exciting, fun and adventurous activities in your life. There will be many places where these things overlap. Just remember, the thing that defines a business is your profit motive. Keep that in the forefront of your mind as you read this book and move forward in your business.

Financial Reality

There are two ways to get ahead financially. They are spend less and make more. Seem too simple? Try naming another way.

Investing is making more. Lowering your overhead is spending less. Reinvesting your profits is making more. All responsible financial activities boil down to these two things.

Most people focus on cutting their expenses. This is particularly true of W-2 wage earners, otherwise known as employees. It's easy to understand why. Once you get a job, you don't want to lose it, so you've got to be careful not to rock the boat. That's what defines the employee mindset. Get a good job and keep it. A good job is one that pays enough, has benefits, plenty of vacation and periodic raises.

That's why most employees focus on spending less. Those periodic raises typically don't cover much more than the increased cost of living, so your salary never really goes further.

You look for sales, cut coupons, and buy in bulk at Sam's Club or Costco. I'm not knocking that at all. Managing costs is an important part of running a business. But here's the limiting factor. The benefits of cost cutting are finite by nature. After all, you can only cut costs so much. Even if you reduced your living expenses down to zero (I've never met anyone yet who has accomplished that feat) you've done all that you can do. More realistically, if you shave off extra expenses here and there, you might be able to reduce your living expenses by 15% – 20%. But that's it. On the other hand, increasing your income has no inherent limit.

Let's look at the numbers. Suppose you make $100,000 per year and live on $95,000. That leaves you with $5,000 in savings each year. (By the way, most people spend 110% of what they earn and go further and further into debt each year.)

By cutting costs and stretching your budget you may be able to reduce your expenses by $10,000 increasing your savings each year to $15,000. Good Job. But if while you do that, you add another $20,000 in income, the net gain is now $35,000. And it's really easy to make $25,000 a year in any business. Of course, the more you make the more the gap widens and the further ahead you are.

Are you beginning to see why you **must** have a business and spend more of your time thinking and planning for the upside potential?

Yet there is a more insidious problem with focusing only on cost cutting. It creates a scarcity mentality. Underlying many people's financial struggle is the subconscious feeling of scarcity. Even if they don't verbalize it, they've learned that there's only so much to go around, and they've got to guard their money diligently. It is true that we've got to be good money managers, but it's also true that if saving or cutting back is our only focus, we can dig ourselves into a rut.

Cutting costs is a left-brained activity. Creating wealth is more right-brained. If you over-develop your logical side, you get out of balance. And in the work of wealth building, the net result is having a poor person's mentality.

Having your own businesses can help you to develop a wealthy mindset—a way of seeing opportunity in everyday circumstances. It's looking at things with an attitude of *"How can I...?"*, instead of *"Why can't I...?"* or *"I can't because...!"* That's what successful people do. In fact, that's all opportunity is. It's solving a problem or finding a different perspective or a different approach. Business people make a lot of money simply solving problems. You can too.

The Rules of Money Are Different for Business Owners

Rule 1: Your income potential as a business person is unlimited.

The first rule we already touched on. That's the fact that, at least in theory, your income potential as a business person is unlimited. Now, let's not get pie in the sky. I'm not saying that you should set your sights on developing a million dollar business in the next five years—if you do, fine, but that's not what we're after at this point.

How about we start with something more modest and build from there. What if we were to take your salary and set a goal of developing half that much more from your own business? So if you make $50,000 that's an additional $25,000, or if you make $100,000, that's an extra $50,000 added to your gross income.

If that still seems like too much of a leap, start with half that amount as a goal and build up to it over time. It's your business and you can grow it as big or as small as you want.

"Did he just say what I think he said? Grow your business small? What kind of book is this? I thought I was supposed to shoot for the sky; dream big dreams; make a million dollars!"

It's great if that's what you want. But I want you to know this: it is your business and you can make it as big or as small as you want. It's your choice—don't let anyone tell you differently.

Rule 2: It's OK to borrow an idea from somebody else.

In school we're told, "Keep your eyes on your own paper or I'll send you to the Principal's office". That's because as school children we understood that borrowing test answers from others is considered cheating.

In the business world it's called a joint venture. Can't write a book by yourself? Work with a co-author or ghost writer. Like to fix up houses but don't like selling them? Get a real estate agent or partner. Love to cook but can't stand the administrative work of owning a restaurant? Work with someone who does.

Joint Ventures make the world go round. Donald Trump uses them. Robert Kiyosaki uses them. I use them, and you should too. They are a way of teaming up and sharing talents and resources.

Another way to legally borrow resources is to create your own variation on the appropriate theme. In other words, your business idea doesn't have to be completely unique. Yet some unique aspect of it can turn it into a whole new business. For example, Dominos Pizza wasn't the first Pizza restaurant or even Pizza delivery service. Yet their promise, "Fresh hot Pizza delivered in 30 minutes or less" distinguished them from the competition and made them millions of dollars in the process.

What unique touch can you add to an existing idea? Maybe it's a special ingredient in a recipe; or a way of improving an existing service or making it more convenient or faster. One of my early clients had a great idea. He realized how inconvenient it can be for busy business people to deal with their dry cleaning needs. So, he started a business that picked up and delivered dry cleaning from the office complexes in the area. He didn't own the dry cleaning facility; he just owned the van that picked up and delivered the clothes to the dry cleaner's customers.

So start looking at existing businesses and put your imagination to work developing ideas that would improve or add to the products or services they offer. Even if you ultimately take your business in a completely different direction, this process will tap into the right (creative) side of your brain and ideas will begin to flow.

Rule 3: The tax laws are far better for businesses than for W-2 employees. Put them to work for you.

Years ago, the U.S. Supreme court observed that there are two tax systems in this country; one for the educated and one for the uneducated. Most people are sadly in the uneducated system. They feel the pain of high taxes (as much as 50%) yet they feel powerless to do anything about it. In other words, **they don't know what they don't know.**

Here are some facts that they don't teach you in high school (or college, or law school):

Being in business can provide incredible tax benefits to you:

- 🕑 **Even if your business is brand new**

- 🕑 **Even if your business is not incorporated**

- 🕑 **Even if your business doesn't make a profit**

- 🕑 **Even if your business has no revenue**

- 🕑 **Even if you've never been in business before**

- 🕑 **Even if you only work at it part time**

- 🕑 **Even if you keep your current (secure) job**

These tax benefits can save you thousands and thousands of dollars each year, even if your salaried income is modest. You must put the educated tax system to work for you NOW!

Rule 4: The retirement plans for business owners are far superior to those for employed workers.

Let's face it, no matter how much you enjoy your career, at some point you want to be able to stop working. My goal is to **not** stop working—total retirement sounds way too boring for me. But it's nice to know that you don't have to work forever, isn't it? Imagine if you could do whatever you wanted with your time, without having to concern yourself with money. If you could go to the office and do what you do just for the love of it.

By having your own business, you gain access to retirement plans that allow you to contribute not thousands of dollars but **tens of thousands of dollars each year** and to invest those funds in virtually any kind of typical investment or business so that it can grow faster than ever.

So, now you know why you must have your own business to get ahead financially. The next step is to begin taking action.

I've learned that in business, recognition and accolades are the booby prize. Not so in our personal lives, but in business, if I get an ovation or a pat on the back, I've failed miserably. For me success means convincing other people to take action. Buy my book, purchase my audio programs, sign up for personal mentoring or invest in one of my workshops.

I want to implore you to take action. Work with this book. Put its ideas to use for you. Put your unique touch to them and use them to make lots and lots of money. Don't just read passively and put it down saying "Wow! That was interesting". Let's work together to create a new financial future for you. Let's do it together. Let's do it now!

Take Action

List 3 benefits of being in your own business that you now understand. Stated another way list 3 reasons why you absolutely MUST have your own business starting now:

1.

2.

3.

If you want to learn more about the tax benefits of owning your own business, call my office at (888) 695-2765 and request a free Action Strategy Session. We'll show you how to legally reduce your taxes by up to 70%, saving you thousands and thousands of dollars each year.

Resources

Books

The Cash Flow Quadrant by Robert Kiyosaki

:01
One Minute Review
Why You Must Have Your Own Business ?

1. Having a business allows you to get ahead financially.

   ↻ The financial rules are different for business owners and non-business owners.

2. The only two ways to improve your finances are to make more money or spend less.

   ↻ Cutting your expenses has inherent limits; increasing your income doesn't.

3. Its OK to borrow ideas from other successful people.

4. The tax laws significantly favor business owners.

5. Retirement plans are better for business owners.

chapter 2

Step 1: Put Yourself on the Fast Track by Working with Mentors and Coaches

> There are only two ways to learn:
> Mistakes and Mentors.
> - Unknown

The Biggest mistake I made as a young entrepreneur was to try to do it all and figure it all out on my own. It was my nature, back then, to be something of a rebel. I was competitive so my rebellious nature served me well, especially in sports. Perseverance, determination and a good measure of toughness allowed me to excel as a young athlete. However, as one of my mentors later observed—for most people, their greatest strength can turn into their biggest weakness. In many ways, that was true for me.

Part of the problem for me was that I was usually busy doing the opposite of what my peers did. In high school, they were busy studying to get good grades. I was busy working at the family business.

In law school, my colleagues were trying to get the attention of the big law firms and to land a "great job". I was committed to starting my own firm—which I did immediately upon graduating and passing the bar exam. And so it went. If most people were going right, I'd turn left. If they went south, I went north.

I was bold and that is a definite asset in business. But at times, I think I had more guts than smarts and my boldness could get me into trouble.

What happened for me is that even with my early mentors, I was brazen and impatient. If I didn't like what they suggested, I'd storm off and do things my own way. I felt like they just didn't understand. Before long, I found myself without any mentors. That's what happens if you think you know it all.

So about ten years ago, I had what I now recognize as a defining moment in my life. I was building a successful law practice on eastern Long Island and I found myself discussing the virtues of practicing law with some of the "old timers" in the area. They told me about how proud they were for having built their own practice to the point where they could support their family in a comfortable lifestyle and put their kids through college. With any luck, by the time they were 65-70 years old, they'd be able to "slow down a little, maybe even retire". Some of these attorneys were working 60 hours a week (I myself was proud of the fact that several of my clients paid me to work as many as 95 hours a week).

All the while, I began to read books and listen to audio programs. I was searching. I knew that something was amiss, but I couldn't put my finger on exactly what it was.

Then one morning it all came together. As I took the long walk from the front door of my office to the mail box it hit me. I stood there on Main Street and looked west. As I did I recalled the earlier conversations with my colleagues about how proud they were for how long and hard they had worked. Then, I looked east and recalled similar conversations I had had with the attorneys whose offices were in that direction.

I Had a Realization.

If I continued on the path I was on, I'd wind up in the same shape they were in. Older, overworked, tired, spending more time telling war stories than planning an exciting future. And it was in that moment that I vowed to find a better way.

I realized that I needed help. If I continued to do it on my own, I would continue to get the same, now unacceptable, results. I had to find others who had found a better way—one that was perhaps similar to what I had in mind, and ask them for direction.

In short, the remedy was to become **coachable**.

I spent the next five years re-tooling. I went to every seminar I could and I listened intently to the successful people that spoke at them. And I started to see a pattern. Many of their stories were similar in that they too had coaches and mentors. The lesson I was learning was that no matter how bright or gifted you are, there are areas where you can learn more and areas where you can improve.

Now there is an interesting phenomenon that I started to observe through all of this. I noticed that my friends and colleagues would at times reach out to each other for advice, but they were asking advice of non-experts. It goes something like this: you're having a problem in your marriage, so you call your best friend (the one who has been divorced three times) and ask for his advice. Or you decide it's time to get into a fitness and nutrition regime and you call a friend who has done a lot of reading on the subject. She may have all the "facts" but unfortunately she is 40 lbs overweight and hasn't seen the inside of a gym in fifteen years.

So the experts seek advice from other experts and the average person seeks advice from anyone who will listen. Are you starting to see the point?

The single most important thing you can do is to seek out Mentors and Coaches and follow their advice. I am always working with at least one coach and one mentor.

The Benefits of Coaches and Mentors

Benefit #1: They'll save you time.

They've been there and done that. They've learned the lessons and already made the mistakes so you don't have to. They have the experience of dealing with the particular issue you're grappling with and they can guide you around the obstacles you're likely to encounter.

Benefit #2: They'll save you money.

Mistakes cost money. I heard a quote recently that said, "There are two ways to become successful: mistakes and mentors". Mentors are much less expensive. Trust me. Listening to my mentors early on would have saved me a half a million dollar loss and all the grief that came with it. They are an investment in your future and if you follow their good advice, that investment will pay off in spades.

Benefit #3: They'll keep you on track.

It's a jungle out there and it's easy to lose sight of your goals. What looks very clear in the comfort of a brain storming session can get fuzzy and distorted in real life. Personalities take over. Money is at issue. There are deadlines.

And don't forget the rest of your life; you know your personal life—relationships, illnesses, friends and family all pulling on you.

Raye was very detail oriented and that made her a great planner. One day she was sharing her biggest frustration—she had lots of great ideas but had been unable to implement them in her business.

I visited her office and she showed me some of the planning "tools" she used. A large erasable calendar divided into 30 day, 60 day, and 90 day goals and tasks, and a color-coded day planner that made it easy to separate and categorize her activities. She even had a journal with pictures of things she wanted to buy and places she wanted to visit. During a 20 minute tour of her office, the problem became apparent. She was spending lots of time organizing and no time implementing.

I proposed a simple solution: Select your most important goal and focus on that alone. I asked her the following question, "Raye, of all the goals and items on your "to-do lists" and journal, what single thing, if accomplished, would bring you the most financial benefit?" She thought for a minute or so and said—"referrals. If I could generate a good referral system, most of my other business problems and concerns would go away."

Then I asked her to list the three things she needed to do to build a great referral system and she did. For the next 90 days she focused on building her referral system and her business has grown dramatically.

Coaches and Mentors can help you navigate your way through real life issues.

Benefit #4: They'll help you avoid BIG mistakes.

I called one of my mentors recently about a new idea I was exploring to promote my business. It concerned creating one day seminars at an investment of $50,000 each. I explained that although I was new at this aspect of the business, I was working with someone who had done similar, though not identical events, so I felt a high level of confidence for our success.

I figured I'd try it once and if it worked out, I would continue. If not, I would cut my losses and drop the idea.

His suggestion was, "Drew, you've got to plan to do at least three or four of those events before you work out the kinks. Be prepared to lose money on the first few." In other words don't do the event if its overall success depends on you getting it right the first time. No one gets anything 100% right the first time through.

Here's what happened. The first event lost over $20,000. We made some changes to the format and the second event broke even. It was only after the third event that we got the system to the point where it made money.

If I had gone with the "I'll give it one try" approach, we would have failed. Planning ahead to gain the benefit of our learning experiences lead to our ultimate success.

Never start something if you can't afford to withstand a few learning experiences.

Benefit #5: They'll help you streamline things.

I just finished a speaking engagement in Vancouver. During one of the breaks, two ladies approached me and asked my opinion about the current state of their business. They had taken several real estate courses, read a number of books, and attended four different "wealth building" seminars; yet they still hadn't purchased their first property. In fact, they hadn't even made their first offer. Sound familiar? It is a very common problem.

They took me up on my invitation to discuss their situation over a cup of coffee. For the first five or ten minutes they expressed their frustration about not getting started and about making a significant investment yet not seeing any return. They shared how their personal situation was getting in the way of their business dreams. In about ten minutes the cause of their problem became obvious:

They we're trying to conjure up and solve every conceivable problem they might face ahead of time instead of taking their first step forward.

Now, I'm a believer in planning and problem avoidance techniques. Yet, may people get bogged down in the "what-ifs" and never get into the game. In just a few more minutes together we outlined a three step plan to get them "unstuck" and on their way to actual real estate investing.

Benefit #6: They'll help avoid frustration.

I don't know about you, but I hate to fail. It annoys me and makes me angry. Yet, I'm an action-oriented guy. I'm not the kind of person who sits around discussing unfulfilled dreams or telling war stories. Early on I was taught that the way to avoid procrastination is to follow this formula—READY, FIRE, AIM—instead of this one—READY, AIM, FIRE—and I took it to heart.

The problem with being so action oriented is that, early in my career, I would wind up shooting myself in the foot. I'd try something and if it didn't work out, I'd try harder. Trying harder isn't always the answer. In fact, if all you do is continue to try harder without the suggestions of a tested pro, all you do is frustrate yourself. The end result of that process is burnout, and possibly many other undesirable consequences.

Benefit #7: They'll offer a different (fresh) perspective.

You may have heard this story. Years ago, a trucker got lost and wound up on the wrong highway. This highway had low overpasses, so when he attempted to pass under one of them, he wedged his tractor trailer right underneath. It was stuck so badly, that no matter how much he raced the engine, he couldn't get it to budge.

The police called in several engineers, a bulldozer and a crane operator. One suggested that they use a bulldozer to pull the truck through. Another suggested that they push the semi back. One of the engineers suggested they use one bulldozer to push from the rear and another to pull from the front. Nothing seemed to work. It looked as if they would either have to cut the truck up into sections and remove it piece by piece or use the crane to dismantle part of the overpass. Neither plan was ideal.

It was around this time that a young boy rode by on his bicycle. After looking things over he called out, "Hey mister, why don't you let the air out of the truck tires?" They did and the truck was liberated!

Sometimes we (and our team) are too close to the situation to see the best solution. It's not just a matter of intelligence or experience. Coaches and Mentors can offer a fresh perspective that can greatly improve the result.

Mentors versus Coaches - Mentors or Coaches

Mentors

Mentors are people with the kind of experience you hope to have some day. They have been there and done that. To be effective they must be at least several steps ahead of where you are already accomplishing what you hope to. Some people refer to them as having a "Dutch Uncle".

For you, they are "big picture people"; they help you plot a course for yourself. They'll point out some of the obstacles you can expect to encounter along the way and suggest ways to avoid them.

Mentors provide guidance. Mentors brainstorm with us.

I usually speak with my mentors (in person or on the phone) once every tow to four weeks. There is no set schedule for our conversation. It happens more or less on an "as needed" basis. We'll discuss a problem or obstacle I'm facing and my mentor provides a suggestion or a different direction to take.

Here's the key—mentors don't get bogged down in details. They are more the "what to do" person than the "how to do it" person. They help us look at a situation from 30,000 feet up and determine what primary elements are needed.

Coaches

Coaches provide a related but different function. Coaches help us work through the nitty-gritty. Whereas a mentor might say, "you need to start investing in real estate", a coach will help you determine what strategy (foreclosures, rehabs, flips or buy and hold) to use.

A mentor might suggest a new stream of income. A coach will help you determine what stream of income would work best for you. A mentor says "you should write a book" a coach says "here is someone that can take you through the process of outlining the chapters, writing it chapter by chapter, doing the cover artwork, publishing it and promoting it."

You'll have regularly scheduled sessions with your coach, typically once a week for 45 minutes to an hour. All of your time with your coaches and mentors should be considered what one of my coaches calls "sacred time". That's time that you can give him or her your full attention, completely uninterrupted.

Get the Most from Your Time with Your Coach and Mentor

Your time is limited and so is your coach's. Nevertheless, I've experienced a number of times when one of my students opted to waste our valuable time together. Come to your session prepared to work. Coaching isn't a casual conversation over a cup of coffee. It is work time so be prepared to work hard.

Some Tips for Getting the Most from Your Session

TIP #1

Determine, ahead of time with your coach, whether your sessions together are to be structured (i.e. your coach has a particular agenda to cover on each call) or free formed (you work together on the particular issue that you find yourself struggling with at that time). Either way, prepare ahead of time by clarifying the particular issues you are going to cover.

TIP #2

Remove yourself from all distractions. Turn off the phone.

Turn off your computer so you won't be tempted to fire off a few quick e-mails. Have a legal or letter size pad of paper handy along with a couple of pens.

- ✪ **Take lots of notes. A good coach can "download" a lot of information in a short period of time. Your mind may be racing with new ideas and one thought will lead to another. Capture everything you can so you can review your notes again and again.**

- ✪ **Ask your coach if you can record the call. If so, use the tape to review the session as soon as possible (it's a good idea to block out extra time in your schedule to do that after the actual session). Then revisit it a few days later and a week later, etc. Your learning will evolve as you do.**

TIP #3

Expect Change. In fact be committed to it. Or as they say in California, embrace change. Your whole point in being coached is to explore what you don't know and put it into action for your benefit. Willingness to try a new approach is a start, but real change requires you to be proactive.

We've all heard the expression that the definition of insanity is repeating the same things and expecting a different result. If a suggestion feels awkward (not illegal or immoral, just awkward) try it.

As one of my speaking coaches says, "There is nothing natural about public speaking. If you feel comfortable in front of a room, you're doing something wrong."

TIP #4

Be Coachable. Think for a moment about everything you already do well. Maybe you're an expert skier. Maybe you're a gourmet chef. Imagine that you're asked to teach a new skier and they struggle over to you, skis crossed, exhausted from the effort of trying something new.

Now imagine that instead of accepting your coaching, the student tells you about all the ski movies he's seen, how his best friend took him down a double black diamond and how he's really a great skier—just a little rusty.

The only person he's kidding is himself.

So, be open to your coach's observations and suggestions. Be willing to give them a good faith try.

Instead of saying...........

    (a) I've always done it this way.
    (b) That will never work for me.
    (c) I've already heard everything you're saying.

Try......

    (a) I can see the possible benefit in your suggestion.
    (b) I'll try your suggestion and see what results I get.
    (c) I've heard that before, now I'll try to implement it.

When I speak live, I tell the true story of my friend Pat. Pat and I grew up in the same town, and went to high school together—that is, when we actually attended. While I was in law school, Pat started his own business and within five years or so, his business was thriving. He was in the enviable position of having at least five strong streams of income.

When Pat and I would get together, I'd warn him about the need for asset protection. He would dismiss it as "seminar stuff". Unfortunately, in about his 7th year of business, disaster struck. Pat found himself involved in a lawsuit. And before long, he had lost everything. His home included.

Had he taken my advice and protected his assets, his losses would have been minor. Instead, because he decided to do things his own way, his losses were devastating.

TIP #5

Implement the new strategies. That's the difference between coaching and casual conversation. Coaching is conversation driven, but action based. It's not a theoretical discussion; it requires implementation. Once you're in motion, your coach can help you steer in a different direction.

How do You Find Great Coaches and Mentors?

Coaching relationships are formal, mentoring relationships can be formal (paid) or informal (unpaid).

If you are looking for an informal mentoring relationship, seek out local business people. It might be someone that is successfully involved in the type of business that you want to get into or just a successful business person that you feel you can relate to. Call them up and offer to buy them a cup of coffee.

Most people who contact successful business people are interested in selling them something or looking for a donation. Few are looking for knowledge. Because of that, in my experience, most prospective mentors are delighted to spend some time with you.

Some tips for your meeting:

1) **Arrive ten minutes early. Whatever you do, don't blow in ten minutes late. The relationship will be over.**

2) **Be respectful of their time. (see #1) Don't *chit-chat*. Get to the point.**

3) **Have a prepared list of questions or topics, and a pad and pen to take notes (I wouldn't ask to record the sessions until the relationship matures).**

4) **If you need specific help, ask for it. They'll respect your directness, whether or not they can deliver.**

5) **Implement their instructions. There is no greater insult in a mentoring relationship than to disregard your mentor's suggestions.**

6) **Be grateful. They don't have to invest their time this way, so YOU pay for the coffee. Don't let them pick up the tab.**

TIP #6

Follow up. After you've completed your action step, send them a note or call them up. Let them know about your progress and request another session for the next steps you should take.

Formal Mentoring and Coaching

If you are interested in a formal mentoring or coaching relationship, contact my office at (888) 695-2765.

Take Action

In the space that follows, write down the 1-3 things that are currently "stumping" you or keeping you stuck:

1._____

2._____

3._____

Now, list five successful business people you can call and request a mentoring relationship.

1.

2.

3.

4.

5.

Alternatively, call my office today at (888) 695-2765 to get involved in one of our coaching or mentoring programs.

TAKE ACTION NOW!

Resources

Books

Mentored by a Millionaire; Master Strategies of Super Achievers by Steven K. Scott

Conversations with Millionaires by Mike Litman and Jason Oman

:01
One Minute Review
Put Yourself on the Fast Track by
Working with Coaches and Mentors

1. Coaches save you time.

2. Coaches save you money.

3. They hold you accountable and keep you on track.

4. They help you avoid BIG mistakes.

5. They help you streamline your efforts.

6. Coaches help you avoid frustration.

7. They offer a different (yet successful) perspective.

8. Don't ask struggling friends for help; use a coach or mentor who is already successful at what you are trying to accomplish.

9. There are a number of ways to find coaches and mentors; it is an investment that will pay off forever.

Step 2: Pick a Subject

Turn your passion into a business.
Turn your hobby into a business.
The more immersed in it you are,
the more driven to success you will be.

Most people who decide to go into business start with this step—selecting what kind of business to get into. In my opinion, that's putting the cart before the horse. That is one reason why about 80% of new businesses fail in the first five years. It doesn't have to be that way.

Some of the confusion arises from the fact that actually operating your business has less to do with the subject (your vocation, calling or passion) than it does with daily operational issues.

In his book *The E-myth Revisited*, Michael Gerber recounts the story of a young lady that loved to bake. When she was young, she always loved the aroma of her grandmother's cakes and pies. Her mother was also an excellent baker and she enjoyed being around the whole experience. Starting from nothing and finishing with a beautiful (and tasty) creation.

Her decision to start her own bakery proved disillusioning. Before long, the business began to take over the baking. She spent more time ordering supplies, doing book keeping and handling customer complaints than she did baking. She was miserable with her bakery. What had gone wrong?

Several things, but nothing that working with a mentor couldn't have minimized or avoided altogether. That's why you need to start there. Assuming you have, its time to pick a business subject.

Businesses fall into two primary categories: products and services. Throughout this book we'll discuss the overlap (hint: all businesses are fundamentally sales businesses; if you don't have sales, you don't have a business).

Early in my entrepreneurial career, I wished there had been a list of possible business types to help get my creative juices flowing. What follows is such a list. The list is by no means exhaustive. Yet by reading through it, you may trigger an idea that will resonate with you and provide a starting point. Also, I've added stories about some of my students who have put a unique twist on a particular business or combined services or products to create a unique business.

The stories are true. Some of the names have been changed to protect their identity.

Products

Product oriented businesses involve the manufacture and sale of an item. You can manufacture it yourself or you can purchase it wholesale from the manufacturer. If you are contemplating your first business venture, I suggest that you stick to selling products that are manufactured by others. The manufacturing process is a business within itself. The overhead and complexity of manufacturing your own product is best avoided in the early stages.

Products
- ↻ **Clothing**
- ↻ **Accessories**
- ↻ **Jewelry**

Case Study #1—Patricia H.

Patricia worked in the entertainment field doing the styling and make-up for actors in television commercials and movies. Using her skill and imagination, she created a necklace she called the "magic crystal". The package came with an imaginative story about how the wearer of the crystal would benefit from its protective powers. She sold it to crystal shops and small boutiques. Later she expanded her line to include custom bracelets and necklaces which she sold on the internet.

- ↻ **Books**
- ↻ **Video Sales /rental**
- ↻ **Thrift Store**
- ↻ **Music C.D's**

Case Study #2—Jeff D.

Jeff is an outstanding musician. His blues band plays weekly at local clubs. He began writing his own music and purchased the electronic equipment necessary to produce his own, professional grade CD.

Soon, other musicians asked Jeff to help them cut CDs of their own and a new business was born.

- ↻ **Electronics:**
  - ● **Computers**
  - ● **Software**
  - ● **Cameras**
  - ● **DVD's**
  - ● **Medical Equipment**

Case Study# 3—Dr. Anthony

Driven by his experience working with people who were addicted to drugs and alcohol, and his interest in technology, Dr. Anthony searched for a technological breakthrough. He reasoned that addicted people had different brain chemistry than the rest of society that caused them to crave their addictions. He searched for a mechanism that could alter their brain chemistry.

After years of research and experimentation, Dr. Anthony had that breakthrough. It came in the form of a little electronic device, about the size of a portable CD player. The patient wears a headset like device which is used to transmit an electrical signal to the brain, thereby altering the brains chemistry.

- ↻ **Sports equipment**
- ↻ **Biking**
- ↻ **Hiking**
- ↻ **Horseback riding**
- ↻ **Skiing**
- ↻ **Write articles**
- ↻ **Write a Book**

- ⟳ **Hobbies:**
- ⟳ **Fishing rods and Tackle**
- ⟳ **Crafts of all kinds**

Case Study # 4—Sue M.

As a teenager, Sue developed an affinity for sewing, often making her own dresses and blouses. As a mother, she made Halloween costumes for her kids and outfits for their plays and recitals. She wanted to turn her love of sewing into a viable business.

A few years ago, she was approached by an acquaintance with a proposition. Her husband designs and manufactures pool cleaning equipment. Each of his cleaning machines requires an on-going supply of filter bags and he needed a local manufacturer.

He produced several samples using different materials and color schemes. The "Boca Bag Lady" was born and she has produced thousands of bags since.

- ⟳ **Woodworking**
- ⟳ **Refinishing**
- ⟳ **Antiques**
- ⟳ **Furniture Making**
- ⟳ **Dollhouses**
- ⟳ **Birdhouses**
- ⟳ **Paintings and Sketching**

Case study # 5—Larry L.

In his youth, Larry showed talent for sketching and painting landscapes. When he was recruited by the Army, they asked for "volunteers" to paint the officers club. Figuring it was better than a lot of the jobs his fellow service men were given, he opted to paint. But what the service had in mind and what Larry envisioned were very different.

They expected a one-color typical serviceman's paint job. What they got instead was a full wall mural of a beautiful country landscape, complete with trees, meadows and a pond. Larry soon became known as "Sergeant Rembrandt".

After his discharge, Larry became a successful businessman. When he retired to Savannah, Georgia, he re-focused his talents on his painting. Several years ago, I spent two weeks with Larry and his wife touring Lake Michigan and the Mackinac Island area. Larry took roll after roll of pictures as we toured.

Later, he set his third floor loft up as an art studio. People began to see his art work and before long, he was invited to display his work in a gallery. Since then, he has been invited into two more galleries and, although his paintings sell for thousands of dollars each, he can't keep up with the demand.

○ Sculpting and other artwork

Case Study # 6—Craig T.

Craig is a free spirit and spends weeks at a time touring the country in one of his four used Greyhound busses.

In his thirties, he developed an interest in body sculpting. After taking several courses and honing his skills, he went to work. He set up one of his busses as a mobile studio and now he travels the country sculpting the hands and faces of local folks—profiting along the way.

Information

We live in the information age. It's no longer a matter of availability as much as manageability. You could provide, organize, research or manage information in any number of areas including:

🕐 **Health**
- **Medical Treatment**
  - **Heart Issues**
  - **Cancer**
  - **Other specific diseases or ailments**
  - **Children's issues like autism and ADD**
  - **Juvenile Diabetes**
  - **Elderly issues**
  - **Altimeters**
  - **Adult Diabetes**
- **Medical Technology**
- **Diagnosis equipment**
- **Treatment Techniques**
- **Chiropractic**
- **Alternative Medicine**
- **Nutrition**

Case Study # 7—Dr. Elizabeth.

Dr Elisabeth is a research scientist with a fascination in nutrition and health issues. While studying for her doctorate, she began to investigate the connection between nutrition, environmental factors and health. For instance, she found a connection between people who lived near chicken farms and cancer. It turns out that carcinogen containing chicken feed leeches into the water supply and, over time, develops into cancer.

She has also uncovered what she calls the "killer gene" which she believes controls the body's time clock. By ingesting a strict regime of supplements and pure foods, her clients can reverse years of damage to the body.

One of her clients was an underdeveloped man in his early twenties. After only a few months of the program, Michael began to put on a healthy amount of weight. Then, something amazing happened. This twenty three year old man began to grow taller—four inches taller in fact.

She works with healthy people as well as the ill. She has helped world class athletes, business people, performers and individuals from all walks of life while building a successful business in the process.

Technology

- ○ **Wealth**
    - **Building and Investing**
    - **Real Estate**
        - ○ Flips
        - ○ Foreclosures
        - ○ Tax Certificates
        - ○ Rehabs
        - ○ Buy and Hold
        - ○ Wrapping

O **Subject To**
O **Land development**
O **Trailer Parks**
O **Commercial Properties**

Case Study #8—Mike Litman

As a young man, Mike Litman was passionate about learning about finances and wealth. In fact, you might say he was obsessed. As the son of a middle class family, he was fascinated by the stories of the Rockefeller's, Carnegies and Trumps. He read every success and personal development book he could get his hands on. As a teenager, he was interviewed on the radio and became intrigued by that medium.

He combined his interest in talk radio with his passion for learning about finances and developed a radio talk show about wealth building and success. Within four years he had interviewed some of the wealthiest and most successful people in the country. People like Tony Robbins, Mark Victor Hansen and Jack Canfield, Wally "Famous" Amos, and the principles of *Rich Dad, Poor Dad*. As he tells the story:

"When I started my radio show, I had three listeners: My mother, my father and one of my friends. But none of my interviewees knew that—I just told them I had a radio show. I was beside myself with excitement over being able to spend time one on one with my idols, picking their brain about their ideas, strategies, marketing methods—anything I wanted. I learned an incredible amount. We taped each show, and over time, the number of listeners grew. Before long, we expanded to the internet and the show was being heard all over the world."

Several years later, Mike and a partner decided to transcribe those taped interviews and turn them into a book, *Conversations with Millionaires*. CWM was born and became a best seller.

A Closer Look

Like most businesses, Mike's has gone through a series of phases. First were the actual interviews. This was really the information gathering phase of his business. It didn't generate any revenue.

Next the first real product, CWM was developed. The book itself became a best seller. Yet, its success opened the door to many other opportunities. Using the model that was perfected by Mark Victor Hansen and Jack Canfield of *Chicken Soup for the Soul* fame, Mike began to conceptualize other "Conversations" books. Conversations with Real Estate Millionaires, Conversations with Network Marketing Millionaires and Conversations with Sales Millionaires are part of the planning.

With the success of the book, Mike himself became the target of interviewers. Stories, articles and radio interviews followed. Mike is also a sought-after speaker. His highly motivational style and resolve not to quit in the early days despite significant challenges, his message of *"Unleashing Your Greatness"* is powerful and practical. You can get in touch with Mike at *www.Greatnessheldhostage.com*.

Investing

- ↻ **Mutual Funds**
- ↻ **Buy and Hold**
- ↻ **Short Term Trading**

- ↻ **Stocks**
- ↻ **Futures**
- ↻ **Bonds**
- ↻ **Music**

Case Study # 9—Carol R.

Carol is a piano teacher who has a teaching studio in her home. A divorced woman, she began teaching music to help make ends meet.

She came to me with a request—how can I use my talent to develop passive income?

We discussed several ideas. She could hire other teachers and expand her existing business. Or, she could write a book on the joys of playing the piano.

Ultimately she decided to develop a special program. The theme: Using the joy of music to get through the stress and pain of a divorce. Her son, who is an amateur videographer, will video the lessons. She'll also provide sheet music and audio tapes in the course.

- ↻ **Fun**
- ↻ **Vacations**
- ↻ **Sports**
- ↻ **Hobbies**

Case Study # 10—Dr. Perry

Dr. Perry is a chiropractor with a very successful practice. He considers his work a "calling" more than a business. He also has a love of horses. He raises and trains them on his backyard farm.

Working together, we helped Perry develop his passion for horses into a substantial business. This made his hobby both a completely deductible expense as well as a source of profits!

- ↺ **Crafts**
- ↺ **Food**
- ↺ **Travel**
- ↺ **Research Books**
- ↺ **Specific Topics**
  - ● **Best Beaches**
  - ● **Best Ski Resorts**
  - ● **Best Golf Courses**
  - ● **Best Hiking**
  - ● **Best Camping**
  - ● **Best conventions**
  - ● **Best Live Shows**
  - ● **Best Concerts**
  - ● **Best Music**

Case Study# 11—Karen L.

Karen loves the adventure of travel. She seeks the unusual and exotic places of the world to visit. Her current interest is castles. Recently, she went on a three week tour of Europe photographing and writing about these incredible historic structures.

In our work together, she learned all about writing and self-publishing a book. Her research (travel, cameras, equipment, etc.) is not only fun, it's a tax deductible expense.

- ↺ **Hotel**
- ↺ **Bed and Breakfast**
- ↺ **Restaurant**

- Delicatessen
- Café
- Examples (selling products on the internet)
- MLM's (Multi-level marketing)

Note: the Internet is a *great* way to launch a business.

Service Businesses

As the name implies, the purpose of a service businesses is to perform a service. Areas include:

- Business Consulting
- Computers
- Electrician
- Plumbing
- Woodworking
- Sewing
- Embroidering

Case study # 12—Patrice N.

Patrice developed a specialized niche with her sewing talent. Seeing that many business people like to display their corporate logo on things like golf shirts and jackets, she began to offer to embroider corporate logos on clothing.

For about $5 per item (more for larger logos) she can do about 15 items per hour. That's $65 an hour for doing something she loves. And, I taught her that putting the logo on clothing makes the total cost tax deductible to the company—a marketing tip she put to good use in attracting business clients.

- ↻ **Handy man**
- ↻ **Carpet Installation**
- ↻ **Carpet Cleaning**
- ↻ **Closet Organizers**
- ↻ **Marketing**

Case Study # 13—Stephen P.

As a short term stock market trader, Steven found himself working on his computer and spending a lot of "down" time waiting for trades to conclude.

He began surfing the web and noticed that more and more companies were using the Internet to sell their products. He learned as much as he could about marketing, especially on the Internet.

Then, he set up several joint ventures with companies that produced products and services he felt he could successfully promote. Not only does Stephen love what he does, he has more than tripled his income with this new talent—all using "down" time.

- ↻ **Bookkeeping**
- ↻ **Administrative Assistance**
- ↻ **Personal Organizers**
- ↻ **Pool installation**
- ↻ **Pool maintenance**
- ↻ **Cleaning**
  - ● **Office Cleaning**
  - ● **House Cleaning**
  - ● **Garage, Attic, Basement Cleanouts**
  - ● **Chimney and Fireplace Cleaning**
- ↻ **Landscaping**

Case Study # 14—Matt Bacak

As a teenager, Matt Bacak had a successful paper route. Over the years, he got to know his customers, their families and even their business travel and vacation patterns. One day while delivering and collecting money from a customer, he realized that the husband's car was not in the driveway. Looking around, he also noticed that the lawn was a little higher then usual.

He offered to return later that day to cut the lawn for a fee of $20. A new business was born.

Within a few months, Matt was busy with his new landscaping business—too busy in fact. So he took the next step. He recruited some of the other neighborhood kids—kids that wanted money to buy baseball cards and music tapes. He offered to pay them $5 an hour to mow lawns, learning that it took an average of 1 hour per lawn making a profit of $15 per lawn per week for Matt. Another entrepreneur was born. Matt has since taken his love of business into many other areas: he is the co-author of a best selling book, a speaker and seminar promoter. You can learn more from him at *Powerfulpromotor.com.*

🕒 **Deliveries**
- **Pizza**
- **Pharmacy**
- **Dry cleaning**
- **Groceries**
- **Packages**
- **Office Supplies**
- **Automobiles**
- **Sandwiches**

Away at college, Mike needed a job that could put gas in his car with flexible hours. We looked for a service that his fellow students needed and would be willing to pay for. We uncovered an interesting fact: every night about eighty percent of the students hung around their dorms studying. Invariably, all their hard work lead to a lot of midnight snacking.

Our idea: offer to buy sandwiches at the local deli and deliver them door to door. He learned that he could buy sandwiches for $5 and sell them for $7.50 each.

- ↻ **Personal Assistant**
- ↻ **Personal Shopper**
- ↻ **Bookkeeper**
- ↻ **House cleaning**
- ↻ **Office Cleaning**

Case Study # 15—Lauren M.

Lauren was in her first year of college and needed some extra money. Unlike many people (myself included) who don't like house cleaning, she enjoys it. In fact she finds it relaxing.

She decided to offer her services to local home owners. I helped her develop flyers which she distributed as an insert in the town newspaper and a small classified ad.

Before long, she had so many accounts that she had to hire help. Money was no longer a problem for her.

MLMs and Other Turn-key Systems

Multi-level marketing (also called Network Marketing) provides a turn-key business system. The system includes the product or service, marketing methods and sales system. It typically also includes the training, brochures, and support required to be successful.

MLMs are now heavily regulated, so the cost of getting started has come down significantly. Some people find that having such a turn-key system makes it quick and easy to get into their own business. Types of business include everything imaginable from nutritional products to legal services, to discount telephone services to pain relieving magnets.

Franchises

Franchises are a more formal type of turn-key system. MLM's provide the system. You must provide, on your own time and at your own pace, the drive and entrepreneurship to make the business a success.

Franchises require a larger investment (anywhere from $5,000 to over $500,000) depending on the franchise. Typically, the higher the investment, the better the franchise track record and the higher the expectation for profit.

Franchisors *require* a certain amount of training and commitment from their franchisees. They have stricter quality controls and require a minimum standard of performance from each of their franchisees.

Franchises like McDonalds are the most rigorous. The investment is very high and the training (at Hamburger University) is long and hard. The franchisor dictates where the store is located, where supplies are purchased and how the operation is run—everything from how long the burgers are cooked to how often the floor is mopped.

Why would a business owner be willing to succumb to such controls? Because the success rate is very high. Virtually no McDonald's go out of business.

Joint Ventures

Joint ventures are a type of partnership—generally set up to accomplish a particular purpose. They are a great way for an entrepreneur to acquire the "missing links" for their business.

For example, you may have a great product but don't possess the skills needed to properly market it. You could J.V. with an internet marketer or direct mail company.

You may have developed a talent for spotting great real estate deals, but lack the funds necessary to complete it. A J.V. with an investor can solve that problem.

The types of join ventures are virtually unlimited. Just identify what your talent is and what's missing to complete it. Find someone else who can provide the missing link to your success.

Hopefully, by reading this list and the accompanying case studies, we've triggered your imagination and helped you come up with some ideas of your own.

Take Action

Write down one or two ideas that interest you. Call your mentor and brainstorm the ideas with him or her.

Congratulations, you're on your way!

Resources

Books

203 Home Based Businesses that can make you Rich by Tyler Hicks.

The Best Home Businesses for the 21st Century by Paul Edwards and Sarah Edwards

101 Best Home Based Businesses for Woman by Priscilla Huff

:01
One Minute Review
Picking a Subject

1. Your Business can be a product or service.

   ◑ Service businesses are usually easier to start and manage.

2. Choose something you have an affinity for; something you are passionate about.

3. The types of businesses are virtually limitless.

4. Franchises and network marketing companies can provide a headstart and a framework. Each comes with inherent pros and cons.

5. Joint Ventures allow you to piggy back on someone else's expertise.

chapter 4

Step 3: The Power of Corporations—Selecting a Structure

An individual with the knowledge of the tax advantages and protection provided by a corporation can get rich so much faster than someone who is an employee or a small-business sole proprietor. It's like the difference between someone walking and someone flying. The difference is profound when it comes to long-term wealth.
-Robert Kiyosaki, *Rich Dad Poor Dad*

Asset Protection - Part I

One of the foundational elements of building wealth is preserving what you acquire. After all, you could spend years working hard to develop your asset base, only to lose it because of one misstep on the part of you or a partner.

A partner? What does having a partner have to do with asset protection? It could have a great deal to do with your overall strategy.

That's because there are many ways of doing business. The first two are the most frequent—sole proprietorship and general partnership.

There are three fundamental forms that your business can take. They are: the sole proprietorship, the general partnership and the corporation.

The Sole Proprietorship

When you run your business as a sole proprietorship, you are the business. You simply "hang out your shingle", print up some business cards and begin conducting business. In essence you, as the owner, and your business are one in the same.

Your assets are the business assets and the business assets are your assets. The same rule applies to liabilities. Your debts and the business debts are one and the same. If your business is sued, it is the same as if you were sued. Conversely, if you are sued personally, your business is sued.

The good news is that it's very easy to get started with this form of business. The bad news is that you have all of the liability should a problem arise. Not only can a claim be made for the value of the business, but the claim can be extended to reach your personal assets. That means that your home, your bank accounts, your car and your personal belongings are all at risk. Everything you own is at risk.

The same applies regarding the IRS. You file one return because all of the income is yours. You pay self-employment taxes at approximately 15.65%. This is true whether you use your name or a business name.

Fictitious Names/dba's (doing business as)

You may choose to adopt a fictitious name for your business. For example, instead of calling your business Mary's Bakery, you may prefer to call it "The Super Fresh, Piping Hot Bakery Stop". It's like using a nick-name for the business.

You adopt this fictitious name simply by filing a fictitious name certificate or "d/b/a" (doing business as) certificate with your County recorder's office. The certificate lists the original name and the new, assumed name.

Some new business owners make the mistake of thinking that the dba certificate provides asset protection. This is a huge mistake—one that can be financially fatal.

When you file a dba (doing business as) certificate, you and your business are still one. Your assets have not been separated from the business, nor are they protected.

I'm not implying that filing a dba is a bad thing. It offers you the opportunity to adopt a new business name for whatever practical or business reason you choose. I'm simply making you aware that there is no asset protection offered by the adoption of a fictitious name.

In summary, sole proprietorships offer no protection and are therefore a risky way to do business. But it can get worse. Bring on the general partnership.

General Partnerships

This is where you and a friend decide to go into business or an investment together. You can do this on a handshake or with a formal written agreement. Either way, this is the riskiest way to conduct your business, all because of something called *joint and several liability*.

What this means is that each partner is responsible for the mistakes or bad acts of the other. Simply put, if you do something wrong, you can be sued. And, if your partner does something wrong, you can also be sued. And yes, your personal assets are at risk. That means that not only is your interest in the business at risk, so are your home, your car, your banks accounts, etc. With a general partnership, this is true even if you have done nothing wrong at all.

Bad enough so far, but it can actually get worse. Say for example, that your partner has a teenage son. One night, the teenager goes to a party, has a few beers and takes the family car for a joy ride. He collides with another vehicle containing two passengers, both of whom are seriously hurt—along with the three friends that were passengers in the family car.

A lawsuit is filed against your partner and his son. If a judgment is entered against your partner, one of his assets is his share of the partnership and before you know it, the assets of your partnership are being attacked and seized by the local sheriff.

In this example, you did nothing to cause the accident. In fact you were sound asleep when it occurred. Yet, because of partnership law, you may find yourself explaining to your spouse why you have to relocate to a new neighborhood.

How should you protect yourself from this problem? Through the proper use of business entities like corporations, limited liability companies and limited partnerships you can sleep at night.

Ideally, asset protection is done in layers. I've heard it referred to as an onion. Each layer protects the one beneath it. Creditors are forced to uncover multiple layers of protection if they even hope to attack your assets, and this process typically proves to be fruitless.

How do You Begin to Protect Yourself?

The first step in asset protection is to separate your business assets from your personal assets. In other words, don't put all your eggs in one basket.

The next step is to separate your businesses and investments from one another. Stated another way, you want to have several different baskets each containing only a few "eggs" or assets.

When protecting assets, I start by dividing the person's asset column in two, drawing a line between their personal and business assets.

On the business side of the equation, the initial layer of protection is a corporation. For virtually anyone in business, this is an essential step. That's because a corporation is a separate legal entity. It can buy property, own property, or sell it as the owners choose. Its assets are separate from your assets so your personal assets are protected from the claims of creditors.

If your business is accused of harming someone, your corporation will stand as a shield. Many people feel that this kind of thing can't happen to them. You have probably heard of the McDonald's case where a customer seriously burned herself when she spilled a cup of hot coffee in her lap. That case reportedly settled for $750,000.

The woman spilled the coffee on herself. It wasn't a situation where one of the employees created the problem. McDonald's only mistake: serving coffee that was too hot.

More recently, a group of people sued Burger King, Kentucky Fried Chicken and Wendy's because the fast food exacerbated their diabetes and caused them to gain weight. Do you think? They are seeking millions of dollars in damages and they are the one's that chose to eat the food! The point is that you can be sued for almost anything, so you must protect yourself.

Special Business Entities

In addition to the unincorporated business entities (Sole Proprietorships, and Partnerships) and the incorporated business entities ("S" corporations and "C" corporations) there are two special forms of business entities that you should know about. They are Limited Partnerships and Limited Liability Companies.

Limited Partnerships are generally used for holding investments such as real estate because they provide extra protection and separate the management of the investment from its ownership. Do not confuse limited partnerships with the general partnerships that we discussed earlier.

Limited partnerships are comprised of two components: the limited partner(s) and the general partner(s). The limited partners are so named because their liability is limited to the amount of their investment. That is to say that if you, as a limited partner, invest $20,000 in a project, the most you can lose from that investment is your $20,000. Even if the project went bankrupt because of mismanagement or if a creditor obtained a judgment for $1,000,000, your sole liability would be limited to your $20,000 investment.

Of course, there are guidelines that the limited partners must follow to maintain that protection. For example, they must not involve themselves in the day to day management of the limited partnership. By doing so, they lose the very shield that the limited partnership was set up to provide them with and their personal assets are put at risk. So, a key for anyone who is a limited partner in any kind of investment is to avoid getting involved in the day to day operations of the venture. Leave that to the general partner.

As you may have already imagined, the general partner has the burden of the liability to bear. S/he is responsible for the day to day management of the limited partnership. In a real estate project that means things like collecting rents, repairing the building, paying expenses, handling the bookkeeping and filing timely tax returns.

So, what can the general partner do to protect herself? When I set up general partnerships, I make sure that the general partner is incorporated. That way s/he has the same shield against liability that corporations provide. As a result, in a properly constructed, properly managed limited partnership, all parties are fully protected.

This leads to another important distinction for the limited partnership. Because the limited partners lose their protection if they participate in the management of the partnership, the limited partnership can be the perfect entity where you want to have "silent" partners. For example, if you want to have complete control over the management decisions of the venture.

Now there's one more very important aspect of limited partnerships. I've heard it said that the best way to win a lawsuit is to avoid it altogether. Here's where the real power of the limited partnership comes into play. It's called a "charging order" and it works like this: if someone sues a Limited Partnership and wins the suit (not an easy task to begin with) their judgment is reduced to what is known as a "charging order". The charging order entitles the victorious party to their pro-rated share of the partnership's profits. However, it also makes them responsible for the taxes incurred by the limited partnership.

Now, here's an example of a creative use of up-streaming income. You can have your limited partnership pay a management fee to a "friendly" (Nevada) corporation. That way, there will be very little to distribute in the way of profits. Yet, the litigant still remains liable for any taxes that might be owed by the limited partnership. The net result is a completely losing situation for the litigant. We will discuss multiple corporation strategies later when we look at advanced asset protection and tax strategies.

Limited Liability Companies (LLC's)

The next tool that we use to protect investment real estate is the Limited Liability Company or LLC. LLCs are the new kid on the block, having been created about 25 years ago. Slowly, each state adopted its own version of the Limited Liability Act and now all states have given them their blessing.

LLCs have several unique features that you should be aware of:

1) **The participants in an LLC are called members, not partners. They are broken down into two types—regular members and managers. For small, closely held LLCs the member(s) is the manager. For larger entities, a separate, third party manager may be brought in.**

2) **Unlike the limited partnership that requires two entities for complete protection (i.e. the limited partnership itself plus a corporation to protect the general partner), the LLC requires only one entity. That usually makes it simpler and less costly to set up and operate.**

3) While LLCs default to being treated as partnerships for tax purposes, they have the flexibility of being taxed either as "S" corporations or "C" corporations as well.

4) Just like the Limited partnership, LLCs are protected by the charging order.

Because of the last three features, LLCs are being used more and more for retail and service businesses, in addition to real estate. So, are Limited Partnerships a thing of the past? No, not really. They still have their place. One situation is when you want control centralized in one person (or entity). Also, some states have an additional tax that they impose on LLCs. So, it's important for us to discuss your particular needs prior to setting up your next entity.

What is the Best Entity for Me?

There is no easy answer to that question, it really depends on the type of business, where it is, the number of "partners" or shareholders and what other entities you may already have. But, here are some guidelines:

Non- Real Estate

If this is your first business, you probably want a flow through entity. That way, if your business loses money during the start up phase (as so many businesses do), you can offset other earned income by the amount your business actually lost. Sole proprietorships and general partnerships are out, because of the horrible liability they expose you to.

That leaves us with "S" corporations and LLCs that have taken the "S" election for tax purposes. Some, but not all states treat

LLCs less favorably, so that will affect the ultimate entity choice. I lean towards LLCs because of the added asset protection resulting from the charging order. They also have relaxed rules concerning the keeping of corporate minutes and resolutions and other corporate formalities.

Real Estate

Historically, we place real estate into a limited partnership; especially for projects where there are passive investors. Limited partnerships provide a clear demarcation of management and ownership, and carry the added benefit of the charging order.

Yet, LLCs also work well with real estate, especially for individuals who are investing by themselves. They provide the asset protection of a separate entity; the added protection and deterrent affect of the charging order and give you flexibility as to the tax effects.

What about Nevada and Delaware Corporations?

Often, after people hear me speak at a seminar, they leave with the impression that they must have a Nevada corporation no matter what. So, let me clear up the Nevada misnomer.

Nevada corporations are important tools for your tool belt, but they are not the end all be all of entities.

Their benefits include:

1) Laws favorable to small closely held businesses

2) Privacy for officers and directors

3) The possibility of bearer shares and nominated officers

4) No reciprocity with the IRS

5) No State income tax, among others.

That's why people like Madonna, Michael Jackson and some of the wealthiest business owners in the country own Nevada corporations.

Yet, there are other disadvantages you must be aware of and consider. These include renewal fees and annual requirements that cost as much as $1,500 - $2,000 and the requirement of a true business presence in the state.

For these reasons, the answer to whether a Nevada Corporation will be advantageous to you, takes careful consideration. Again the type of business and where it is truly located are important issues. For example, California residents would like nothing more than to shift income out of the onerous California State tax system over to tax free Nevada, but the State of California is particularly sensitive to that strategy. You can't just deposit in-state income into a Nevada corporation and expect to shield it from your state income tax structure. Yet, there are ways that you can legitimately reduce your taxes using Nevada Entities.

Closely related is the issue of "S" vs. "C" corporations. Students often ask me if they should have an "S" corp. or a "C" corp. as if they have to choose only one. As your asset column grows and evolves, you will undoubtedly need more than one entity. So, there is little doubt that, at some point, you will want to utilize a Nevada corporation, but it may be a bit further down the road. The ultimate question is which entity(s) will best serve you now for your current business purpose. Often, the answer is, in part, a matter of timing.

Take Action

Call my office to schedule a free session with our entity strategists who will assist you in selecting and setting up the proper entity.

Resources

Pathfinder Business Strategies Mentoring Program which is available by calling (888) 695-2765

:01
One Minute Review
The Power of Corporations-Selecting a Structure

1. There are different forms your business can take:

    a. Unincorporated Forms:

        i.. Sole proprietorship.

        ii. General Partnership

    b. Incorporated Forms

        i. "S" corporation, "C" corporation

        ii. Limited Partnership

        iii. Limited Liability Company

2. Business entities provide asset protection and tax benefits

3. Certain forms work better for particular types of businesses than others.

4. Having multiple entities can be very advantageous to business owners

5. Get professional advice when selecting your entities.

chapter 5

Step 4: Make Some Noise
The Importance of Sales and Marketing

> If you have a valuable product or service, then you are
> ripping people off if you *don't* insist that they buy it.
> - Mike Litman

How Important are Sales and Marketing to Your Business Success?

They Are Essential.

Fundamentally, business is simple. And it all starts with sales. Without sales there is no business. You may have a great hobby. You may have a passion or pastime. Yet without sales, you don't have a business. And if your marketing is poor, your business will suffer.

One of my first businesses after leaving the protective nest of my family's building supply business was my law firm. I've shared with people that unlike most of my classmates, my desire in law school was not to land some cushy six figure job with a big law firm; I had no interest in that. Truthfully, I couldn't understand their reasoning behind going to school for seven years for the primary purpose of working for someone else and making them wealthier. I thought they were nuts (This was in the days prior to Robert Kiyosaki's book *The Cash Flow Quadrant*). I just couldn't relate.

During law school, I also started my real estate investing. I spent many of my weekends driving out to my properties where I worked from early Saturday morning till late Sunday evening framing, sheet rocking, spackling, painting, etc. in order to build or spruce up one of my rental units. (Oh! Can I tell you some stories…..)

So, I graduated law school, passed the bar exam, and immediately began the practice of law under the name Andrew Miles and Associates. In those days, the "associates" consisted of a couple of my law school friends that helped me out in their spare time —why do you think they call it "practice". No one was the wiser. So off I went into the tough world, too foolish then to know any better. In fact, I had more guts than brains. Yet, I digress.

It Takes More Than Expertise

During this time I met an incredible attorney named David. To this day, David is the most competent, well versed attorney I've ever known.

You need to understand that today, the practice of law, like many other professions, requires specialization. The days of the one stop shop family attorney finally ended in the 1980's. There is simply too much to know to be a general practitioner. Attorneys must concentrate on a particular area of the law.

David seemed to know more about every area of law than even the "specialists". Ask him a question about criminal law and he'd give you the answer. Ask him about commercial litigation, he'd give you the answer. Torts, Family Law, Matrimonial—it didn't seem to matter. He would cite statutes and case law and invariably, after following up with our own research, his opinion would hold up. Now, David did have his area of specialty, but he was what is known as a "lawyer's lawyer". As such, he was an incredible resource to our fledgling firm.

With all that expertise, you'd think that David would be wealthy, or at least that he had a thriving practice. Not so.

Long before I even knew it, this was my first lesson in marketing.

You see, instinctively I knew that I needed new clients in order to stay in business (the word instinct as used here refers to the intense human desire to pay the rent and eat three meals a day). So, I aligned myself with other attorneys. I soon learned that every attorney has a few cases they just don't want to deal with—for whatever reason. Sometimes it's a difficult client, sometimes it was an area of law outside their normal scope of practice.

I solved their problem by taking over their unwanted files and I grew my practice at the same time—with a set of built-in advisors and mentors to keep me (and my clients) out of trouble.

Back to David.

Despite his incredible amount of knowledge and years of experience, David always seemed to struggle financially. In those days, I couldn't understand it. Now, the problem is obvious.

Knowledge does not equal wealth. Expertise does not equal financial success. Technical competence does not equal cash flow. Only a steady source of new and repeat customers generates cash for the business and there is only one steady source of new and repeat customers: sales.

Sales are the lifeblood of a business. Without sales, the business withers and dies.

I've heard many a business person say "I don't like sales" or "I'm no good at sales". Invariably, I can guess their income within $10,000 and it's usually very low. Incredibly, I've had students tell me that the only reason they went into a network marketing business was to avoid having to be involved in sales. Yet, sales are what network marketing is all about. MLM companies are turn-key businesses with only one component missing: you guessed it—sales. If they had the sales, they wouldn't need you.

At one point, David decided that what he needed was a new "image". He hired a professional consultant to help him re-create himself. He tossed the eyeglasses in favor of contact lenses (these were the days before Lasik surgery). He adapted a new, more glamorous hair style and he got a completely new wardrobe. In truth he looked a lot better—certainly more professional. But his business didn't improve at all. Not one bit.

Get Your Name Out There

Compare that to another example from the legal community that was occurring at the same time. J&M were California attorneys with a talent for marketing. In their view, what was needed was-n't simply more lawyers, it was affordable legal services. So they built their practice around that concept.

Before long their office grew and expanded to a second office. The firm didn't handle complex matters—just simple family issues, personal injury and "Mom and Pop" type business matters. Even newly sworn in attorneys could be quickly trained to handle these matters. And law schools were pumping out new attorneys by the tens of thousands each year, so supply wasn't a problem. They simply added more staff attorneys to handle the additional cases.

Then they had a huge breakthrough. They realized that what they had created was a turn key business system. Everything from the marketing and sales, to handling each kind of case had been systematized—that the only way they could handle the large volume of cases at "affordable" prices—they realized they could go national.

Within a few years "Jacoby and Meyers" was recognized by blue collar Americans as the law firm for working families. They made millions.

What was the difference between David and Jacoby and Meyers? Both firms offered the same type of services. David had more expertise. David was recognized by his colleagues as an authority. David was a better lawyer. Jacoby and Meyers were better at sales and marketing.

They found a niche and put the word out. In the 1980's they advertised on T.V., radio and magazines. You'd even see their ads on billboards around the country. Few people knew about David.

The Lesson

Most new business people spend inordinate amounts of time "perfecting" their product or service. Their mistake is in thinking that sales will take care of themselves. That's a fatal mistake.

I'm not saying that quality is not important. Quite the contrary; you must continually seek to improve and add value. Yet, successful business people launch their business knowing that they will have to "course-correct" and they do so *while* building their business.

Let's take a lesson from the airlines. When an airplane sets out from New York to Los Angeles, it doesn't travel in a straight line. The pilot guides it in the right general direction, yet things like air traffic, wind and weather blow it off course. The actual flight path looks more like a zigzag than a straight line. In fact, I've heard it said that airplanes are off course over 90% of the time. Yet, they typically reach their destination—and on time at that. How can that be?

It's simple. They constantly course-correct. If the wind blows them 2 degrees to the right, they steer 2 degrees to the left and so on, all the way across the country and across the world. And that's not just flights that have gone awry, either. That's all flights. Every single airplane must be course-corrected during every single flight. Its part of the plan and it needs to be part of your plan, also. (This is where your coaches and mentors come in).

The point here is not to let the fact that everything is not perfect prevent you from tooting your own horn.

How Can You Make the Most Noise?

This is not a book on sales, so I'm not going to go into an exhaustive discussion of sales techniques. There are hundreds of great sales books and programs (I've included some resources at the end of this chapter).

The sales process can be broken down into two steps:

A. **Lead generation: i.e. marketing - the process of bringing people into your sales funnels; and**

B. **Lead Conversion: i.e. the sale. This consists of uncovering the person's pain and offering a cost effective solution.**

The goal isn't always to make the most noise; it's to make the best noise for your market. So, step one is to determine who your market is. In other words, develop a niche.

It's a common mistake for new business owners to say, "My product can benefit everyone, so I'll market to everyone". If your target is everyone, chances are your message will reach no one. So, the process goes something like this:

I sell a product that teaches "how to" manage real estate tenants.

Initial Thought: my market is everyone interested in investing in real estate—too broad.

First Refinement: my market is all real estate owners—still too broad.

Second Refinement: my market is all multi-unit owners and people thinking of becoming landlords—better but still too broad.

Third Refinement: my market is all actual landlords—perhaps.

Forth Refinement: my market is all landlords with problem tenants. Good!

Fifth Refinement: my market is all landlords who have evicted a tenant who damaged their property—still ok, but probably too narrow.

Sixth refinement: my market is all landlords from New York City who have evicted a tenant who damaged their property— unnecessarily narrow.

From the above, probably the forth version is the best niche for you. It's easily identifiable. You can reach (contact) these individuals (just get a list from courts of every landlord who has started an eviction proceeding in the last 3 to 6 months. You understand their problem (pain) and you can solve it (the information in your course.).

Now that you've identified your niche, how do you get the word out?

There are lots of ways to generate leads for your business. Because every business is different, you must find the "mix" that works best for you. Notice I said "mix"—the implication being that you should use more than one method to generate new leads. Here are a few ideas to consider:

1) **Newspaper ads**
2) **Magazine Ads**
3) **Classified Ads**
4) **Internet Marketing :**
    a. **Search Engine performance**
    b. **Banners**
    c. **Classified internet Ads**
    d. **Develop a great list**
    e. **Affiliate programs**
    f. **Develop an eZine**
5) **Flyers**
6) **Free Samples**

7) **Public Appreciation Days**
8) **Self Publish**
9) **TV**
10) **Cable TV ads, infomercials, "still" ads**
11) **Signs**
12) **Billboards**
13) **Broadcast e-mails**
14) **Direct Mail**
15) **Post Cards**
16) **Electronic Post cards**
17) **Voice Auto dialers**
18) **Newspaper feature**
19) **Press release**
20) **Grand Opening**
21) **Discount Coupons**
22) **(Tape, article, newsletter) of the month Club**
23) **Knock on doors**
24) **Free evaluation**
25) **Public speaking**
26) **Introduce yourself and shake hands**

Some of these strategies require expertise to be effective. For example, copyrighting (the process of writing an effective sales letter or ad campaign) is a special area of expertise. There are people you can hire just to right your copy and there are books and courses you can study. Why?

Because the difference in results between a well worded sales letter or ad and a poorly worded one can be 500% or more. You have the same product and same level of service, but your letter sells $1000 and the expert's pulls $500,000. That's why.

One of my coaches gets paid $5,000 per day (about 6 hours of work) to review my presentations. The first time I did that presentation, I sold $2,000 worth of product. After making the investment for his services, I did the same presentation one week later and made $20,000 in sales. Same service, same level of my expertise—a 1000% gain in revenue. That $5,000 investment will make me millions in just a few years.

So, you have to know your strong points and outsource your weak points.

Some of these strategies require no expertise. For example, a few years after starting my law firm, I moved it to eastern Long Island. It was a new area for me. There were several "old timers" with established practices and I had to get my name out there. Two things made all the difference in the world—one by "luck" one by design.

I rented a house while deciding whether to build a place and the realtor that showed me the area asked me what kind of law I practiced. When I told her "real estate" and "business" she said, "I want to introduce you to the other sales people in my office."

Fifteen minutes later, she had arranged an impromptu meeting of all 8 sales agents. I introduced myself, shook hands and promised to give any clients they sent my way the royal treatment. Then, without any request from me, she called the other three real estate offices in town and arranged meetings for me with them!

To this day, I don't know why Victoria extended herself that way for me, but the client referrals from those offices formed the backbone of my law firm until I retired from the practice nine years later.

The second "technique" was equally simple. I vowed that every morning and every afternoon, I would visit one deli and one restaurant and have a cup of coffee or a bite to eat. During each visit, I introduced myself to the owner, manager or several of the customers. No hard sell, just a handshake and my business card. Within 2 or 3 months I had to stop my visits because I was too busy handling all my new clients.

It doesn't have to be hard or fancy. Just pick a strategy and stick with it for a while—one key thing to remember when choosing a marketing strategy is to be consistent.

Joint Ventures

Don't Forget Joint Ventures. Joint Ventures are another way to outsource your weak points.

There are lots of ways that you can use joint ventures to your advantage. Earlier, we explored the situation where you had no product, but were willing to do the work selling it. In these cases, you've got the product and you need help selling or marketing.

Remember David?

Here's how David finally solved his problem. He formed a partnership with two established attorneys. They had the client base, he had the expertise. It was a match made in heaven (or at least as close to heaven as three lawyers working together can get).

I'm doing that on the Internet right now. I realize that there are dozens of ways to effectively market on the net, and that my time is valuable and limited. So, I've set up joint ventures with several people, each with their own particular strategy or expertise. My sales increase, they generate revenue and the new customers are thrilled to have access to my products and services. Everybody wins.

Sales is just a word that describes letting people know how you can solve their problem quicker, better and less expensively than someone else. And it's a learned skill.

Commit to learning and using a few new strategies this month and I'm confident you'll see a difference in your business.

Take Action

1) Identify your best niche

2) Launch your product—you'll course-correct based on the feedback you get from customers and prospects

3) Choose three examples from the lead generation strategy list above and implement a lead generation strategy around each; consider combining two or more into an even more powerful strategy

4) Consider a JV partner

Resources

Programs

Unleash Your Greatness by Mike Litman
Greatnessheldhostage.com

The Powerful Promoter by Matt Bacak
Powerfulpromoter.com

Books

Ultimate Selling Power by Dr. Donald Moine

The Ultimate Marketing Plan by Dan Kennedy

Getting Everything You can out of All You've Got by Jay Abraham

The Ultimate Sales Letter by Dan Kennedy

:01
One Minute Review
Make Some Noise- The Importance of Sales and Marketing

---

1. Technical competence alone does not equal success.

2. Selling is a process. Learn it by going step by step.

3. You can build your marketing system over time and in stages.

4. There are lots of effective ways to market your business inexpensively.

5. Networking (formally and informally) is a great tool.

6. Joint ventures can jumpstart your sales and marketing efforts.

chapter 6

Step 5: Systems

The cornerstone of every successful business
is systems.
- Michael Gerber

When Billy G. came to me, he was about to throw in the towel on the idea of being in his own business. He was exhausted from overwork and worry and he could barely make ends meet. Then, there was the paper work—buying supplies, paying employees, collecting outstanding invoices. What's worse, he just returned from a meeting with the IRS and learned that he owed them sales tax. They gave him 30 days to pay up, or they would file a lien against him personally. He told me that he was ready to "give up and just take a job with another landscaper."

Billy had started his landscaping service while he was in high school. After classes, he had enough daylight to cut one or two lawns and on Saturday he could devote the entire day. His little business grew by word of mouth, one neighbor to the next.

Initially, he pushed his lawn mower from job to job. Once he got his driver's license, he used his old pickup truck to cart his growing inventory of equipment. Slowly he purchased more tools: rakes, shovels and a thatcher. When his business could justify buying a leaf blower, he felt he had reached the big time.

By the time he came to see me, he had two trucks, both with trailers, two power mowers and his crowning jewel—a brand new riding mower. Not the typical "homeowner" type that looks like a small tractor. This was a dual steering job that he could maneuver around trees and shrubs.

He had over 100 accounts, 2 full time employees and 2 part time employees. Yet he was working longer hours and making less money than when he worked alone. He was disgusted and fed up. Not just with his business, but with business in general. And he was ready to quit.

During our first meeting, I could see that Billy needed to just talk. He felt like no one understood what he was going through. His wife kept telling him to get a job—or what's worse, "get a real job". He couldn't explain that he loved his business; he just couldn't stand it when things "got out of control". He tried hiring different employees. At first, that seemed to help. One or two of them seemed to be real stars, but before long—it was business as usual.

I said nothing for 45 minutes. At last, Billy sat there quietly. I asked if there was anything else he felt he needed to tell me and he said, "No, that's it. I'm done." He was looking down at the top of my conference table, obviously dejected. I think he meant he was done with the business, but I used the opportunity to ask him a question.

I asked, "Billy, if things weren't out of control, would you rather be in your own business or work for someone else?"

He looked up and gave me an expression as if to say haven't you been listening to me for the last 45 minutes? I assured him I had heard everything he said and I re-asked the question.

He thought about it for about 15 seconds and said, "I don't want to work for anyone else. I love being in my own business. But maybe this is the wrong business for me, maybe if I was in a different business......."

"Wait a minute, cowboy, I said. I heard everything you told me earlier. Now it's my turn to speak and ask the questions." He gave me a knowing grin.

So I continued. "Imagine that your business was completely organized. Everything worked like clockwork. Supplies were ordered timely, employees were properly trained, customers paid you on time and you had time off scheduled each and every week." He looked at me as if to say, "Are you kidding? That would be great!" Then the doubt returned and he said, "Yeah, but it will never happen."

Then, I asked him the defining question. "Are you willing to commit the next twelve months to restructuring your business so that it is profitable, fulfilling and leaves you with personal time to enjoy your family?" He thought about it for what seemed like a few minutes and said, "I am, if you can promise me it will all work out." I replied, "I can't promise that your whole life will suddenly be perfect, that you'll lose fifteen pounds or that you'll have the body of Arnold Schwarzenegger. I can promise that I will teach you what you need to do to gain better mastery of your business, and perhaps your personal life in the process. You need to commit to taking the necessary action."

He extended his hand and said, "You've got a deal."

The Business Isn't the Problem

You see, I knew from experience that Billy's problem wasn't unique to him. In fact, it's something every business person struggles with to some degree. The problem isn't the business; the problem is the way he was *running* the business, or rather, the way the business was running him. In truth, the problem was him.

It happens to the best of them. You start a new business and you feel like you can handle it all. You get a few customers, handle the books, provide the service, and order the supplies. It keeps you busy, but it's pretty manageable.

As the business grows, you can keep pace with it—for a while. Here's what happens. You get a little better and faster at balancing the check book and ordering your supplies. In fact, you've got it down to a phone call where you call the supplier each week and just say. "It's me—give me the usual". You realized that if you wore a headset while making your phone calls, you can return e-mails at the same time. In between e-mails, you can pay a few bills and have lunch at your desk.

As you "improve" you find you can also pick up the kids at school in between phone calls and start dinner. Back to your desk for a few minutes, pop on the headset and make a few calls while the roast is in the oven and the water is coming to a boil. When you've really got it down, you can do it all while going to the bathroom.

Then, one day it all goes south. You get a few too many e-mails and there are 27 messages in your voice mail, your hard drive crashes (did someone say "backup") and the kids (customers, suppliers, etc.) are a little late. The water boils over and the toilet backs up and suddenly you're standing in your bathroom with your headset on, up to your knees in .... Well, let's just say your whole day went to crap.

Systems are the Only Way

Michael Gerber is the godfather of business systems. I read his book The *E-Myth-Revisited* years ago when I was struggling to manage a growing law firm. What intrigued me was the fact that not only does virtually every small business suffer from a similar disease, but that the solution is universal.

Every business needs systems. The precise systems are different but most of the general areas are similar. For example:

- **Lead Generation (marketing)**
- **Lead Conversion (sales)**
- **Product Development**
- **Operations**
  - **Product Delivery**
  - **Product Returns**
- **Financial**
  - **Accounts Payable**
  - **Accounts Receivable**
- **Customer Relations**
- **Customer Satisfaction**

The mistake that most new entrepreneurs make is that they think the business is only about the subject matter. Lawyers think their business is about the law. Mechanics think it's about fixing cars. Pilots think it's about flying.

But your business is about so much more than that.

Gerber uses the story of a bakery owner to make his point. He describes how, as a young lady she becomes fascinated with her grandmother's baking. Every weekend, the smell of fresh baked bread and cakes wafts through the house. That sweet smell lifts her spirits and before long her grandmother is teaching her how to bake for herself.

Years later, she starts her own bakery. It isn't long before she becomes disillusioned with all the other tasks that have to be done to keep this business running. She's so busy ordering supplies and making deliveries that she doesn't have time to do the very thing she loves, bake. Pretty soon, she's ready to throw the muffins and her customers, right out the door.

- ⏱ **Systems convert chaos to order**
- ⏱ **Systems convert frustration to deliverable expectation**
- ⏱ **Systems bring reliability**
- ⏱ **Systems improve performance**
- ⏱ **Systems allow consistency**

Systems make your business enjoyable and fulfilling—for you and your customers

Every franchise business has a set of systems which must be followed. If you don't follow the systems, you lose the franchise. Why, because the franchisor has spent years and hundreds of thousands of dollars developing systems that work.

Can you imagine taking over a McDonald's and replacing the "special sauce" with your own recipe? You'd be dis-enfranchised (thrown out) in two seconds.

That's why you pay so much for a good franchise. Because the systems have been developed and perfected over time. In other words, the franchisor is telling you to invest not only in his product (Big Macs) but also in his way of delivering those products (Golden Arches, Ronald McDonald, golden French fries, a clean, family setting, etc.) He's saying use our product and follow our systems and you'll make money. Fail or refuse to follow them and you'll lose money (and your franchise).

Bill Z. came to me at the end of his franchise career. He had owned and operated a Dunkin Donuts franchise for about 3 years and he was done. He was selling his business, simply because he wanted out. He was tired, unshaven and smoked 2 packs of cigarettes a day. His hands shook and he could barely make decisions. He looked 20 years older than his 55 years.

I can remember him telling me, "It's not like they teach you in donut school. If you follow their way of doing things, you'll be out of business in a month".

Now, I don't know if that's true. What I do know is that Bill would have been better off physically and emotionally if he had left the business after a month. You see, he didn't like to follow their systems. He wanted to make up his own systems.

Get in a little earlier. Stay a little later. Do things just a little differently.

You know what happens if you add the ingredients for a recipe in the wrong measure or order. You get mush instead of a soufflé. Bill got mush and a lot of it.

That's one reason that franchises aren't for everybody. You've got to be willing to accept and implement their winning formula, instead of discovering your own.

I bumped into Bill about 6 months after we closed on the sale of his business. I hardly recognized him. Thankfully, he was more relaxed and rested. He looked a decade younger then when we had met. He had started his own business and it seemed to be much more to his liking. You could see the difference in his face.

What About Network Marketing

Network marketing businesses (MLM's) have a more relaxed set of systems. Essentially, the parent company is saying we've got a great product (or service) that we'll allow you to sell for us. We'll make sure the product is high quality, and we'll give you a formula for success.

We'll even support you with ongoing meetings, teleclasses, and marketing materials (flyers, brochures, a web site, etc.). If you follow our systems, you should make money. If not, we can't be sure if you'll make money or not. We won't take away your right to sell our stuff, but you may not make any money either.

They give you more flexibility—to succeed or fail as you choose.

The problem for most people who get involved in MLM's is that they don't realize that they are, at their core, sales organizations. The company supplies the product or service and it's your job to sell it. It doesn't matter if its phone cards or pre-paid legal services, supplements or office supplies. You must sell stuff to succeed. Unfortunately, many people get so wrapped up in the excitement that they miss the fact that the whole thing is about sales. And they seem surprised six months later when the hype has worn off and they haven't made any money.

No sale, no income. It's that simple.

Where Do I Start?

So Billy and I began working together that spring. The first thing that we did was to identify the areas of the business that were causing him the most difficulty. Gerber calls it the Key Frustrations Process.

I asked, "OK Billy, what three things about the business cause you the most grief. Let's just get them down as you think of them— we'll prioritize later."

Billy answered, "I told you, it's the whole thing—my employees don't show up, my customers pay me late—and then complain about my service and..."

"Let's take it one step at a time", I responded. You see, one of the key things about cleaning up a business is to separate it into its component parts. Then, identify the problems within each component and solve each problem—one at a time. Often, by solving one problem, you solve several others in the process. That's a bonus.

So, I asked Billy what the single most frustrating thing was about the business. After some deep thought, he said, "Not getting paid on time by my customers. I'm there, week after week and sometimes it takes me a month or more to collect. It messes up my accounting, I pay my bills late and my employees still want their paycheck on Friday. It's got to change." And change it did!

So, I said, "Let's design a system that encourages your customers to pay on time, rewards those that pay early and gets rid of the bad payers. Is that a fair goal?"

"But, if we get rid of the bad payers, I won't have any customers."

"Let's see about that," I said.

So we went about it in steps. Phase one was to encourage customers to pay on time.

Phase One - Reaching Out

I suggested that we design a letter to all of his customers. The headline read "Act now to avoid a price increase". It explained that the costs of delivering his service were rising, and that one of his biggest business costs was financing late payments.

So, to reward the customers who paid on time, he was deferring the ten percent price increase. "Mr. and Mrs. Jones, this will save you $20 per month—over $200 per year just for leaving your payment check in your mailbox every Friday morning." The letter went on to explain that he would waive the additional charge if they forgot once—it wasn't his intent to penalize well intentioned customers.

Then, I asked Billy what it would cost him to spray a little miracle grow on his customers flower beds. He calculated the cost at about $3 per house, including the time (less than one minute) it would take one of his men to do the spraying. We calculated this as a $20 value.

So the letter went on to explain that Billy was instituting a pre-payment bonus program. Every customer who paid for the full month's landscaping service ($200 - $250) would receive free flower fertilizing for the entire month—an $80 value absolutely free.

Immediately, his on time payments went up by 50%. Much to his surprise, 20% of his customers began to pre-pay and their flower beds, of course looked outstanding. They had the biggest and prettiest flowers in the neighborhood.

Slowly, he began to weed out his later paying customers as part of Phase 2.

Phase Two - A Shift of Focus

Billy said his next frustration was attracting new customers. "And half the ones I get, pay late anyway", he complained.

I asked Billy how he got most of his new customers. He showed me his Yellow Book ad and a flyer that was inserted in the local newspaper. One of the problems I uncovered was that the customers were from all over the area. In other words, he had to travel as much as 20 minutes between jobs to reach some of his customers.

We devised a plan. We determined that it would be better to have more customers in a particular neighborhood. We also realized that most people aren't particularly loyal to their landscaper. About 40% will switch services if you give them a good reason. We also realized that the cost of providing the service was less than half of the usual fee charged. In other words if Billy charged $50 his actual cost was about $20, including the fertilizer for the lawn and the flowers.

Lastly, I asked Billy how long it would take him to make a new customers lawn and flower beds noticeably improve. His response was 3-4 weeks for significant improvement.

Here's the plan we came up with for Phase 2:

Billy put together a new Flyer. This one started with, "I'll give you Free Lawn care for the next month". It went on to explain that although he had been in business in the area for many years, he hadn't had the opportunity to improve many of the lawns in the neighborhood. In order to encourage new business, he was offering one free month of lawn care—if you are totally satisfied with my service, I'll continue at the price of $55 per week, prepaid for the month. If you are not totally satisfied, you owe me nothing.

In order to avoid an avalanche of new business, I suggested that Billy only distributed 100 flyers at a time. He got special coveralls for himself and his men that had "Billy's Lawn Services" stenciled on the back—clearly identifying the business to potential customers.

He knocked on doors, introduced himself to the neighbors, and explained his services as he handed out the flyer. Twenty-five people took him up on his offer. Twenty became permanent customers.

Let's look at the costs and benefits of this campaign.

Cost:
Twenty five lawns at a cost of $20 per week for 4 weeks = $2,000

Return:
Twenty new customers at $35 profit per week for 52 weeks = $36,400

That's $36,400 profit for a $2,000 investment. And that's just the first year. Calculate the profits if you keep those customers for 3 years, 5 years and 10 years.

And the added bonuses: all pay on-time, many pre-pay for the month and all the new customers are in the same neighborhood —many are within walking distance of each other making the commute between jobs a matter of a minute or so instead of driving across town in traffic.

Phase Three - The Employees

By now, Billy knew that several of the employees would have to be replaced, but he wanted to retain as many as possible. After all, many of them were hard workers and he wanted to give them a chance to fit into the "new" business.

So we met one evening for coffee and started our session by identifying three key problems he was having with his employees. The first was that they would show up late for work several times a week. Because he had six employees, he and the other five would have to wait around until the last one arrived. That cost him a bundle in wasted salaries and time.

Next, their performance on the job was sporadic and inconsistent. We realized that everyone had good days and bad days, but sometimes their work was so shoddy, it seemed like they didn't care. It was affecting the quality of the overall job and the level of customer satisfaction.

Lastly, he found it hard to attract the best possible employees. The most talented and hardest workers often went to the bigger landscaping customers because their jobs seemed more secure with the "big guys."

Here's what we decided. First, Billy instituted a penalty/bonus system to ensure on time arrival. Each time you were late, you got docked $5, and if you were late three times in one week, you were sent walking. The $5 didn't cause them serious financial hardship, but it was enough to get their attention. It stung financially and psychologically to get docked. He also implemented a policy of buying lunch for the employee who was on time the most each month. This worked like a "trophy" or service medal of honor—lunch with the boss each month. The last part of the system really won the day.

He realized that all of the employees had cell phones. If they were late, he would call them and have them drive right to the job instead of meeting up with him to travel as a group. Because they weren't driving a big truck and trailer, they often arrived at the job site before him. The tardiness issue improved. Now that most of Billy's clients were within walking distance of each other, his employees could walk from job to job. Because of this fact, his employees could avoid getting the inside of their cars dirty with grass clippings and landscape debris. Both Billy and his employees benefited from the use of cell phones and the close proximity of clients.

To improve performance, he instituted another penalty/reward system. Every time a worker "scalped" a lawn, caused a brown spot, or left weeds in the flower beds, they were penalized $1. This heightened their awareness and caused them to pay more attention to the details of what they were doing. He also gave a $20 bonus to the worker with the overall best performance and attitude during the month. After a few months, he developed a written "scorecard" with ten different criteria and he scored them three times each week. That added feedback kept the employees involved in the process. Performance began to soar.

The third problem, attracting the best workers available solved itself. Billy's Lawn Services was now growing faster than any of his competitors. In fact, they were losing accounts to Billy. His workers were doing a better job, and the lawns that they tended looked noticeably better. Landscaping laborers were now calling Billy asking if he had a job opening.

In three months, we were able to turn Billy's whole business around. The irritations were gone and it became fun again. In fact, he enjoyed a new sense of pride because everyone was noticing the difference, including friends, family, customers and competitors. He was now running his business instead of the other way around.

In the ensuing months, we continued the key frustrations process. We applied it to his book keeping and record keeping system. He hired a bookkeeper, switched everything over to Quick Books and began to keep impeccable records. His checking account was balanced, his accounts receivable was reduced to zero and his bills were being paid on time.

We found that he had been dramatically overpaying his taxes. We went through the process of converting many of his "personal" expenses into deductible business expenses and saved him over ten thousand dollars in the process. We also separated his growing asset column and protected him with corporations, limited liability companies and trusts.

By the end of our first year working together, Billy and his business were entirely different. Both were energized, proud, and actively adding value for customers.

We met one last time in the late fall and I suggested that in our second year together, we would take on the next level of challenges. Billy said, "But Drew, everything is great with the business. I'm making more money than ever. My business has almost doubled and my customers and employees are happy. What else could we possibly do?"

I smiled and responded "Billy, there is always more you can do. Systems need updating, some improvements don't last forever. Your equipment needs repair and maintenance. We've stopped the bleeding and the patient is doing well, but we can't stop now."

"Besides, do you think your competitors are going to take your new-found success lying down?"

"What do you mean—I built my business fair and square and if they lost some customers in the process, that's their problem", said Billy.

"Fair and square for sure, Billy, but don't expect all of them to just sleep through the winter complacently. They will do what they can to re-coup those customers—to win them back and away from you."

I could see the look of concern in Billy's eyes. I said, "Not to worry, my friend. We'll be working hard this winter also. The next system we are going to design is "Billy's Client Satisfaction and Retention System"— the one that will keep the customers coming back for more—year after year." The twinkle returned to his eye and I could see the recognition.

This was a team effort and we were a team. Business and customer loyalty is not something to take for granted. You have to earn it again and again. So, after a short vacation that's where we began our next level of work. Billy's business continued to prosper and he remained in control.

He continued to add customers; we expanded his focus to include additional streams of income; we set up a retirement plan and insurance for himself and his family, and an estate plan. The "before" and "after" pictures were an amazing contrast and Billy was enjoying the fruits of his hard work.

You Can Screw Up Systems

Occasionally, I'll begin working with someone who has things twisted around. They'll say things like, "Yeah, but I can get around that system." or "You can't make me follow that system." as if systems were a lock to be picked or an obstacle to overcome.

Systems are part of the solution. But like any beneficial process, if you ignore them or cut corners, you won't get the same results.

It's like a diet or nutritional plan. If you're more dedicated to disproving its validity then you are losing weight and getting in shape, you'll prove your point. You'll win the argument (battle) and lose the war.

So, don't make the system the bad guy. And if you've got employees who have a similar approach, you may have to replace them.

Start Slowly

People resist change. That doesn't make them bad, it just makes them people. So start implementing your systems slowly. Don't go into the office Monday morning and expect your staff to memorize and follow thirty seven new systems. Start with no more than one or two. See how the employees respond. See how the customer responds. See how the business responds.

In fact, one of your systems might be "tongue and cheek" titled "The System Implementation System".

Before you add another new system, you may have to tweak one you've already added. Slow and steady. Step by step. This is a marathon, not a sprint to the finish.

Before long, you and most of your employees will embrace the new systems. They'll see and enjoy the positive results. Most people want to be part of a winning team.

Those that don't will have to leave. It will become obvious to you.

Systems Must Evolve

As your business grows, the systems will evolve. Steps will be added. Others will be removed. New systems will be designed and others will be retired. Again this happens over time and is a very natural occurrence.

When McDonalds started out, it was pretty much hamburgers and cheeseburgers. Then they added the Big Mac. Years later, it was the McFish. Then Chicken McNuggets and now green salads. And so it will go for you.

- ⟳ **New products...**
- ⟳ **New services...**
- ⟳ **New systems...**
- ⟳ **Enjoy the process!**

Take Action

List and describe the three most problematic areas of your business:

1.

2.

3.

Perform the Key frustrations process on each of these areas and develop a system (s) to solve any problems identified.

Resources

Book

The E-Myth Revisited by Michael Gerber.

:01
One Minute Review
Systems

1. A lack of business systems can make your business a nightmare.

2. Proper systems can make it run smoothly and reliably.

3. As you identify problems with your business, design systems to solve them.

4. Each area of your business can be systematized.

5. Franchises and Network Marketing companies come with built-in systems.

6. Start with your biggest, most frustrating problem. Systematize the solution and expand to other areas.

chapter 7

Step 6: Get Your Finances in Order

A Penny Saved is a penny earned.
-Ancient Proverb

Many new business owners have a tremendous, (yet unfounded) fear of handling business finances. I have some good news: if you can balance your personal check book and keep decent track of your personal expenses, you can handle the requirements for keeping business records. And if you can't balance your personal checkbook, just hire a bookkeeper.

This chapter is not intended as a comprehensive and detailed study of accounting. It is designed to give the new business person a place to start. If you follow the principles I discuss, you'll be in great shape. As the business grows, you'll want to delegate the bookkeeping to a full-charge bookkeeper (see the chapter on delegation). In the meantime, this is what you need to get your business off to a great financial start.

As a youngster involved in the family business, I remember my mother handling the bookkeeping. Those were the days of manual "crank" adding machines and manual typewriters. The PC hadn't yet been invented. There was even something she called the "posting" machine. It had nothing to do with the mail. It was the machine that she used to prepare the monthly statements for our customers. It was this monster that had its own stand; it must have weighed 200 pounds.

It had all kinds of dials and attachments and sounded like a combination of a coffee grinder and an old used car. Mom would roll it out at the end of each month and I'd steer clear of it. I had an idea of its purpose, but I wanted nothing to do with it. I'd much rather operate a forklift or tractor. They were simpler and less dangerous to operate.

It's much easier today. Computers have replaced the old bookkeeping equipment and the software that's available for about $100 could track the finances of a small country. You've got it easy!

Where to Start

There are several keys to handling your business record keeping. The first is keeping complete and accurate records. The second is separating the business from your personal finances—let's start with this part first.

Some people make the mistake of running their business from their personal check book. This is a mistake for two reasons: from a tax planning perspective it's too easy to lose valuable business deductions when you lump all your finances together. From an asset protection standpoint, it leaves the door open for a creditor to claim that you and the business were in fact one entity, not two. This gives them the opportunity to "pierce the corporate veil" and make claims against your personal assets.

That's very bad and also completely unnecessary.

Here's what I suggest: first, open a business checking account at your favorite bank. If you're doing business as a sole proprietor (perish the thought) you can file a d.b.a. certificate, giving the business its own name. That name should appear on the account and on your business checks.

Next, run to the nearest computer store and buy Quicken or QuickBooks. There is other bookkeeping software available, but these are the most commonly used. They are easy to learn and most accounting firms are familiar with them. You probably don't need the latest version or the one with all the super duper features. Buy last year's version and save yourself $50. You can upgrade later, if necessary.

What's the difference between Quicken and QuickBooks? In a nutshell, Quicken is an electronic checkbook. It allows you to print checks, add deposits and balance your check book. It can even provide you with simple reports.

QuickBooks is a complete bookkeeping package. It does everything that Quicken does, plus provides full financial statements. It has lots of components and add-on modules to handle more complex accounting. It's got everything you need and more.

That doesn't mean it's more difficult to use or learn. I think it's just as easy, and the added features are there for you or your accountant to use when you want. For that reason, I'd take the plunge and buy a one or two year old version of QuickBooks to get started.

It will save you many, many hours oo tedious work.

The first 5 years I was practicing law, we did our own bookkeeping—manually. That meant that we hand wrote every check and reconciled the accounts by hand. The adding machine and printed tape were always close by. That was bad enough.

But, preparing our year end information for our C.P.A was a total nightmare. You see, your accountant will need a general ledger prepared in order to complete your tax returns. That means taking a large ledger sheet and making a separate entry for every deposit and every check that was written during the year. As the firm grew, we wrote more checks.

The last year of our manual system I decided to make this tedious task more tolerable, so I set myself up at a table in our living room with a T.V. set near by. I watched football all day Saturday and all day Sunday; then again the next weekend and again the next. It took me over 45 hours to manually prepare our stuff for our accountant. I got to see a lot of football that year, but I swore I would never put myself through that torture again.

We immediately switched to QuickBooks. The next year I did the same job by pushing a button and sending the print command. 5 minutes versus 45 hours. You decide for yourself.

Your Chart of Accounts

Many people are unnecessarily intimidated by the chart of accounts. Let's make it simple. There are income accounts, expense accounts as well as equity and liability accounts. Forget about the equity and liability accounts for now. Let your accountant worry about those. Let's just focus on the income and expense accounts.

Every expense your business has and every deposit you make

has an associated account. It's not a separate bank account; it's more like a bookkeeping folder. It's a way of linking each expense and each deposit with a specific category.

Deposits might go in to the income account for sales or service fees. An expense might be linked to the "Utilities" account or "Auto Expenses". The chart of accounts is simply the list of all of these accounts.

How do you set up this chart of accounts? More good news: QuickBooks will do it for you. In fact, when you run the program for the first time, it will ask you a few simple questions about your business. Is it a service or sales business? Are you on a cash or accrual basis? (Go with cash basis, it's almost always cash basis).

Then, the program will generate your first chart of accounts. They are so similar from one small business to another they've designed a template that will work for you. You or your accountant can always add to it or subtract from it. Don't worry about making a mistake you can't correct. There's no such thing.

If you want some coaching on getting QuickBooks up and running, you can buy a book like QuickBooks for Dummies or a CD from "the Video Professor". For real diehards, there are live classes available in high schools, colleges and computer stores.

Additional Business Accounts

Your main business checking account is called your operating account. That's where your income is deposited and where you pay your bills.

I also suggest you set up a separate checking account called your tax account. It should say "Tax Account" on the account title right under your business name.

One mistake new business owners make (here, "new" means anyone who has been in business for 20 years or less) is not setting aside enough to cover their taxes. Now, keep in mind that one of the things that I teach people is how to legally minimize their taxes. We all have to pay our fair share of taxes. The key is to pay *only* your fair share, and no more.

Sometimes, a student will tell me, "Drew, I don't want to pay any taxes at all." And I remind them, "They have a special place for people that pay no taxes. They give you three meals a day, your own place to live and a complete (though limited) wardrobe."

So we all have to pay taxes but the problem comes between March and April each year. It goes like this:

Jan started a new business investing in real estate. All year long, he was busy running his business—finding properties, advertising and showing them and doing all the "fix-up" work needed to sell the property. Here's the good news. By the end of the year, all his hard work started paying off and he had a profit of almost $100,000!

He got his records together and in February he met with his accountant, Lenny. A few weeks later, in mid March, his accountant called him and said, "Jan, I've been working on the information you gave me and I want to congratulate you. It's only your second year in business and you had a great year. I've done all my calculations and I got your taxes down to only $30,000. So, drop by my office, sign your tax return and make a check payable to the IRS for $30,000."

Jan said, "Well Lenny, that seems a little steep. Can't I pay it off over time?" Lenny said, "Actually Jan, you were supposed to pay it as you went along last year. You've got to get that check into the IRS immediately. But that shouldn't be a problem. After all, you had about $100,000 in profit!"

"That's true, but I spent that money. I mean, I had to pay my mortgage, and groceries, then I had some doctor bills, clothes, and other living expenses. I only have $5,000 in the bank."

Can you see the problem? The problem is that Jan is living on money that doesn't belong to him. And the IRS doesn't like to wait for its money. They expect to be paid on time. So, to encourage prompt payment of taxes, they have several tools. They are called penalties, interest and a tax lien. And, over time those penalties and interest can be so steep, that they can add up to more than the initial amount of taxes. And, before long, they'll file a lien against you that ensures that they get their money (and destroys your credit rating).

It doesn't have to be that way.

What I want you to do is to set up a separate tax account. And every week, take some of your profits and set them aside into this account. That way, when your taxes are due, you can simply write a check. Your C.P.A. can help you figure out how much to deposit into the account every week.

No hassles. No worries. No penalties, interest or tax liens.

Special Accounts for Some Businesses

Some businesses have certain significant expenses that are vital to the business and should be earmarked in a separate account. These are expenses that are inherent to your business and necessary for it to exist. Yet, the timing of these expenses may be uncertain.

For example, one of my businesses sets up corporate entities (corporations, limited Partnerships and limited liability companies) for people. There is a fixed cost for each of these entities that must be paid. I may collect $1,295 from my customer, yet I know that at some time, I will have to pay for filing fees, expediting, printing, binders, assembly, delivery, etc. Sometimes, it takes several weeks for my customer to return the completed application after placing the order. Yet, I know that when the order comes, my business will have to pay those costs. It's not a question of if, it's a question of when and how much.

So, I set up a separate account I call my "Inc." account and for every order, I immediately transfer enough to cover the cost of the entity out of my operating account and into the "Inc." account.

When I had my law firm, we had a separate disbursement account. When we took on a new client, they would pay us a retainer, plus a certain amount toward things like court filing fees, investigators reports, appraisals, stenographers, etc. These amounts were not fee income to us, so we separated them into a different account.

The account serves two important purposes. First, deposits made into that account are not income to you. You should not be taxed on money that is not being earned by you as income.

Also, by separating these funds from your operating account, you are certain that the money will be there when it's needed to pay for the proper expenses. I have seen business people mistakenly spend expense money because it was commingled with their operating money. This can create all kinds of havoc for your business.

Some Examples:

> ✪ **A landscaper might set aside the cost of shrubs, trees and sod for an upcoming job**

> ✪ **A mechanic might set aside the cost of an engine or transmission**

> ✪ **A boat or car dealer may set aside the cost of the vehicle**

> ✪ **A dentist may set aside the cost of a crown or veneer**

> ✪ **A contractor may set aside the cost of the materials (lumber, brick, stone, hardware, etc) needed to complete a job**

Lastly, I'm going to suggest that you set up one more account. That's your saving or investment account. You've probably heard the expression "pay yourself first". For years, I didn't understand what that meant or how to do it. So, this is how you pay yourself first.

Each week, you take a pre-determined amount and deposit it into a savings account. It might be between 5% and 10% of your anticipated profit. Over time that account will grow and provide you with the means to make other investments. After all, if you are not setting aside some savings, what are you going to retire on? Social Security? Forget it! You have to provide your own retirement plan and this is the first step.

Keeping Complete and Accurate Records

By using QuickBooks, you've taken a big step in the right direction in terms of record keeping. Yet, there are still a couple of more things to do.

Each year, my bookkeeper, Mary, sets up folders for each type or expense the business has. There's a folder for utilities, auto expenses, rent, travel, etc. The folders follow the chart of accounts pretty closely.

Each time she gets a bill, she pays it, writes the check number and date on the written invoice, and files it in the appropriate folder. For example auto expenses—at the end of the year, she has every auto expense we paid that year in one place, one folder.

At the end of the year, she sets up new folders and starts over again.

Bank Statements and Cancelled Checks

We keep the monthly bank statements for each checking and savings account in separate folders. After the account is reconciled each month, we file the statement in the appropriate folder and keep the checks in numerical order (depending on the number of checks you write per year, the stack can get quite high).

Audit Proofing Your Records

There are just two more steps you must take to audit-proof your records. The first is to notate your receipts and keep them. The second is to enter certain types of receipts into a tax log or diary. For example, expenses like travel, meals, entertainment, and auto expenses, while deductible, require an extra step.

Here's what we do. If I take a customer out to lunch and we discuss business, the cost is fifty percent deductible. The key is to log the answers to five distinct questions: Who? What? When? Where? How Much?

I pay for the meal by my business credit card, and make a notation on the receipt something like "Ted T. regarding Jacksonville seminar." Three of the questions are answered on the pre-printed receipt; the other two are in my note. When I return, I give the receipt to Mary (I hate paper work and she's a great organizer) and she transcribes it into a tax log. It looks something like this:

Who	What	When	Where	How Much
Ted T.	Jax Seminar	5/3/04	Joe's Rest.	$32.50

Mary actually set it up in a color-coded excel spreadsheet, but you can use a table like the one above, a ledger book, or a yellow pad. It doesn't have to be fancy it just has to be accurate.

This isn't meant to be the definitive guide to corporate books and records. It's a great starting point and if you follow the guidelines I've laid out for you, you will be off to a great start and your accountant and bookkeeper will have what they need to make the necessary adjustments as you move forward and grow your business.

Take Action

1. Purchase Quicken or QuickBooks (You can get older versions at a discount from Computer Magazines or On-line). Commit two hours of your time to learning its basic functions.

2. Set up your operating account, savings account and tax account.

3. Interview several local bookkeepers and choose the best one for your needs.

4. Contact my office at (888) 695- 2765 to request my free CD "How to Build Your Wealth Team".

:01
One Minute Review
Get Your Finances In Order

1. You must separate your business finances from your personal finances.

2. Get set up with Quicken, QuickBooks, or some other electronic bookkeeping program.

3. Set up an operating account, tax account, savings account and escrow or trust account, if needed.

4. Keep accurate records and documentation to audit proof your records.

chapter 8

Step 7: Effective Time Management

The problem is that most people major in minor things.
-Anthony Robbins

As a business person, you will experience growing pressure on your time—new customers, products, bookkeeping, marketing, administration, customer satisfaction, sales, quality assurance and on and on. You will inevitably be pulled in many different directions at once. The only solution is to learn to effectively manage and balance your time.

Lori and I sat down over a cup of coffee. She was feeling stressed and frustrated. Her husband was busy running the family restaurant (about 16 hours a day) and she had several important business projects she was involved in—a curriculum for teaching kids how to become financially free, a thrift store that she created to raise money for her church, her normal teaching duties and a special project she was working on outside her regular school district which required her to fly to a nearby city once a week to teach. Oh, yeah, then there was her family who no doubt would have preferred to spend more time with "Mom".

I remember telling her, "Lori, I've got good news for you. I just had a heart to heart with God and he's promised to extend the normal 24 hour day by 3 hours. So, beginning Monday, we'll all have 27 hours each day to accomplish all our good work!"

Learning to effectively manage your time is paramount to your success; you will not be as successful (financially, emotionally, spiritually or in your family life) if you don't. The good news is that there are some tools to make the job much easier.

Keep in mind that each one of these tools can be, and in fact is the subject of books, tape sets and seminars. I encourage you to go into each one more deeply. My purpose here is to outline the tools that I have found most useful in my own life. Some you've heard of already and you may benefit from a new perspective. Others will be new and you may want to add them to your existing tool belt.

Goal Setting

The fact is that most people spend more time planning their wedding and vacations then they do their life. As a result most weddings and vacations are well orchestrated, fun and joyful events and most people's lives are in varying stages of disaster. With a road map, you can find your way anywhere. Without one, you'll be lost before you know it. A well thought out properly organized set of goals is your road map.

The cornerstone of effective time management is to understand clearly what you want to accomplish. Otherwise you can be very efficient with your time, but you won't be very effective. In other words if you are completing unimportant tasks twice as fast as before, you are being more efficient, but you are not heading in the right direction. And going faster and faster in the wrong direction won't get you to where you ultimately want to be—right?

Decades ago, a remarkable study was done involving one hundred Harvard graduates. Twenty five years after each one graduated, they interviewed each of the students in order to determine how much they had accomplished. Each had similar backgrounds and resources and had received a similar level of education. The conclusion: the three people with written goals had accomplished more than the other 97 combined.

That is the power of having well thought out, written goals.

Learn to Visualize

The starting point for effective goal setting is to spend some quiet time alone and in a comfortable setting. Sometimes I'll use my office, close the door and shut off my phone while other times, I'll go to the beach or to a park. It is essential that you have at least 30 - 60 minutes of uninterrupted time, preferably more.

When I lived in New York, I'd often go to my cabin on 40 acres of secluded land and sit overlooking the pond. Occasionally I'd get a visit from a humming bird or a family of deer. Their input was always appreciated.

Bring a pad and pen (or laptop computer) and get alone in a relaxing setting. Let your mind wander. Play comforting music or light a candle if that helps you. Just let the events of your day go and settle into a relaxed state.

Here's how you can organize it. Take one page for each of the major areas of your life including your business, relationships, spiritual life, health and fitness, education, fun and adventure, workshops and seminars, community service. Make that area the heading of the page.

Then insert sub-headings on the page for 10 years, 5 years, 1 year, and each quarter. Leave sufficient space between each section.

It will look something like this:

Category - Goal	Action Step
FUN/ADVENTURE	
Within 10 Years	
Have Visited 5 Countries	
Raft on 5 Level 5 Rivers	
See Hawaii and Alaska	
Within 5 Years	
Visit Hawaii	
Raft 1 Level 5 River	
Visit 2 New Countries	
Within 3 Years	
Ski Europe	
Balloon Ride in Sedona	
Bike Europe	

1 Year	
Camp in Grand Canyon	
Sailing in Caribbean	
Bike 100 Miles	
Last Quarter	
Bike 100 Miles	
Workout 4x Week	
2nd Quarter	
Visit Nat. History Museum	
See *The Producers*	
1st Quarter	
Jazz @ Waterfront	
Test Local Bike Path	
This Month	
Get Bike Serviced	
Workout 3x /Week	
Buy Needed Camping Gear	
This Week	
Get Bike Out of Storage	
Find Old Camping Gear	
Find Interested Friends	
Today	
Start Working Out	

Category - Goal	Action Step
BUSINESS	
10 Years	
Net Worth $2 Million	
5 Streams of Income	
5 Years	
Net Worth $ ½ Million	
2 Streams of Income	
Own Office Building	
3 Years	
Regularly Making $200 k	
Business Fully Systematized	
1 Year	
Marketing Systems in Place	
$100k Gross; $50 k Profit	
100 New Customers	
70% Retention	
Last Quarter	
New Ad Prepped & Ready	
Media Selected	
2nd Quarter	
Ad Firm Selected	
Ad Designed	

1st Quarter	
Interview Ad Firms	
Interview Telemarketers	
This Month	
Learn More About Print Ads	
Research Ad Firms	
This Week	
Read 2 Advertising Books	
Learn About Marketing	
Today	
Do Scheduled Coaching Calls	
Call, Fred, Mike and Matt	
Buy First Advertising Book	
Call Mentor About Advertising	

Begin asking yourself questions like: Where do I want to be in ten years? Where will I live? What will my house look like (a center hall colonial, Tudor or contemporary beachfront house)? Who am I with? Am I married (with kids…if so, how many)?

Maybe you want to travel, or perhaps you like to stay home and throw parties.

What kind of car are you driving—a sports car or an SUV? Is it air conditioned or do you have the convertible down? Do you prefer a stick shift or an automatic transmission?

How much money are you making? One million? Ten Million? $200 thousand? What's your net worth? How many employees do you have and what does your office look like?

Go through every major area of your life asking similar questions about your business, relationships, spiritual life, health and fitness, education, fun and adventure, workshops and seminars and community service.

Spend five to ten minutes on each of these areas and just write down what comes to you. It's not important if it seems unlikely or impractical. The key at this stage is to just write it down.

For those items that are more complicated or multi-step, you may want to list individual action steps that you'll need to take. For example, if your goal is to sail the Caribbean in a 30 foot sloop within 12 months, you'll need to get a passport, locate the right travel company, set aside sufficient funds, ask some friends to join you (or not), etc. You can list each of the action steps in order of importance in the space provided.

Invariably, somewhere during this process Mr. or Mrs. Doubtfire will appear and begin telling you why your dreams are unachievable, even ridiculous. I suggest that you smile at him/her, thank them for sharing their thoughts and go right back to what you were doing. Don't get into a wrestling match with your internal naysayer. Don't evaluate or analyze. Just keep on dreaming and writing. There will be plenty of time for practicality later on.

Continue with this process for each area of your life for each of the time frames listed.

You'll probably want to switch over to a word processor for the next step if you haven't already. Take each of the goals that you've listed and rearrange them in order of priority.

Which is the most important goal in each category, the second most important goal in each category, the third, etc? Can you see that your life is starting to come together in a new and more powerful way?

Know Your "WHY"

Now for the power step—experiencing the underlying reason why each goal is really important to you. It's one thing to make a list of goals. It's quite another to really get in touch with them; to walk with them and try them on for a time before committing yourself to the time and energy required to achieve your goals. My friend John DiLemme calls this *"knowing your why"*.

For each major goal, ask yourself why it's important to achieve it. Stay with the question for a while, delving deeper and deeper. Why is it important to become a millionaire (assuming it is)? Is it the pride you'll feel, the cars you'll drive, the neighborhood you can live in? Maybe it's to prove yourself, or to provide special opportunity to your family. Maybe it's to retire to do community service or support your favorite charity. Keep repeating the question asking "what else" as new answers reveal themselves. You may find that what really motivates you deep down surprises you. When you're sure that you've gotten to the bottom of it, write it down in a new column labeled "My Why". Now, your long term planner looks like this:

Category - Goal	Action Step	My "Why"
FUN/ADVENTURE		
Within 10 Years		
Have Visited 5 Countries		
Raft on 5 Level 5 Rivers		
See Hawaii and Alaska		

It's a good idea to review your entire list for internal consistency. For example, if your goal is to have a net worth of $5 million within five years and under the 3 year goals you've listed net worth of $6 million, you've got an inconsistency. Conversely, if your 3 year goal is to have a $5 million net worth and your 1 year goal is to increase your income to $100,000, you've got a different kind of inconsistency. It's *incredibly* important to make your goals realistic and consistent. Otherwise, your subconscious will go to work against you.

Here's a good guideline for setting each of your goals; choose a comfortable target for each one, and raise it by 5% - 10%. That way it's a stretch without being intimidating.

Once this process is done, I transfer my daily action steps to a separate sheet. You can do this to summarize the goals in all your major life areas into weekly, monthly and quarterly goals and action steps.

I prioritize each item using a dual system. I call it the *ABC, 123 System*. The first step is to categorize each item into its first level of importance. The most important action steps (these are usually business items) are labeled "A", the next most important are "B" and things like chores are labeled "C". Within those categories, you will prioritize each item with a 1, 2, 3 etc. depending on its level of importance within the larger category. So, the single most important thing for you to accomplish today is labeled "A-1", the next most important item is labeled "A-2". The least important thing to do that day might be "C-5" or "C-10" depending on how many items are in the "C" category.

Mary Kay Ash (of Mary Kay cosmetics fame) is an extremely successful business woman. She said that one of the keys to her success was to select the six most important things to accomplish each day and to complete them in order of importance. Then, she was finished for the day.

In other words, success isn't a matter of accomplishing everything you can think of. It's a matter of accomplishing the most important things. Once you have done so, you are through for the day. As you develop the skill of identifying the most important things to accomplish, you can work fewer hours, because the busyness goes down, while the impact of each item goes up.

My daily action list looks like this:

PRIORITY	ACTION STEP	PROGRESS
A-1	Call Mark re: Website	
A-2	Schedule Next 3 Day Seminar	
A-3	Call New Promoter Re: Speaking Engagement	
B-1	Read Fourth Chapter of Marketing Book	
B-2	Buy Mari Flowers	
C-1	Pick-up Dry Cleaning	
C-2	Buy Groceries	

One way to determine whether an action item is an "A", "B" or "C", is to use the **priority quadrant system**. It looks like this:

Urgent	Non-Urgent
Important	**Unimportant**

Using this system, each potential action step gets categorized two ways: Urgent vs. Non-Urgent and Important vs. Unimportant.

So, every task falls into one of the following categories:

- **Urgent and Important, or**
- **Urgent and Unimportant, or**
- **Non-Urgent and Important, or**
- **Non-Urgent and Unimportant, or**

Let's use these criteria for the items on the above daily action step list:

Urgent and Important—"A's"

- 🕑 **Call Mark re: Website**
- 🕑 **Schedule Next 3 Day Seminar**
- 🕑 **Call New Promoter Re: Speaking Engagement**

Non-Urgent and Important—"B's"

- 🕑 **Read Fourth Chapter of Marketing Book**
- 🕑 **Buy Mari Flowers**

Urgent and Unimportant—"C's"

- 🕑 **Pick up Dry Cleaning**
- 🕑 **Buy Groceries**

Non-Urgent and Unimportant

- 🕑 **Clean-out My Closet**
- 🕑 **Get Dog Food**

When you compare the items in the priority quadrant to those in your daily "A,B,C" list you'll see clearly how they fit together.

Things that are urgent and important (in other words the most important), high impact action steps for you to accomplish are "A's". Things that are non-urgent and yet are important are your

"B's". Things that are urgent and unimportant become your "C's". These are usually the fires that must be put out. And the things that are non-urgent and unimportant don't even make it onto your daily list. Forget about them for now. It's not that things like cleaning the closet are not ever going to get done; it's just that they don't need your attention now. Maybe you cleaned out the closet a few weeks ago, and while it's not pristine, it's not sloppy either.

Or maybe, you are in the midst of a big business push right now and you need to be focused more on business items. Whatever the reason, these items are excluded from your daily list.

The best time to prepare your daily list is at the end of the prior day. I leave my office at 6 pm so I prepare Tuesday's list on Monday from 5:45 to 6:00. Monday's list is prepared on Friday afternoon. I find that by doing this, my subconscious mind begins to work on these tasks overnight. They "percolate" and often by the next morning, I've found a solution or streamlined my approach significantly.

You've taken the time and energy to put together your daily road map—now follow it. In other words, start with your "A-1", and work on it until it's complete. Then, move to "A-2" and stay with it until it's complete. Avoid the urge to jump around and knock off the quick ones. You'll wind up spending your valuable time on low priority items. Focusing on low priority items leads to a low priority life. Get it? Train yourself to focus on the high-impact "big ticket items".

An Interesting Pitfall

Years ago, I introduced this system to my office and before long I saw my employee's productivity go up significantly. Things that formerly took a week to accomplish were now taking one or two days—former monthly tasks were being completed in a week. But my partner looked more and more distressed with time. A few weeks into the process I said, "You seem to be struggling with the new time management system—what's wrong with it?" She rolled her eyes and said, "There is no way I can get ahead using this system. In fact, every day that goes by, things get worse. I'll never catch up!"

Sensing something was off I asked if I could look at her daily action list. Immediately I found the problem. Next to every single item on the list was the notation "A-1". In her mind, everything was so important that she labeled it "A-1". With forty seven "A-1's" she didn't know where to start. No wonder she was stressed!

So, remember there is only one "A-1", one "A-2", etc. Just complete them in order of priority and you'll be well on your way. Review your progress after one month and you'll be amazed at the results.

I Just Can't Get It All Done—The Art of Delegation

At some point in your business (sooner rather than later), you'll reach a point where you just can't get all the "A's" done. If your "A's" are truly money making items (and in business, they should be) then you'll need to start delegating. Here's the best description of delegating I've heard: You can't afford to do $15 an hour work if your time is worth $50 per hour. And you can't afford to do $50 an hour work if your time is worth $150 per hour. And so on.

So, as your time becomes more valuable, start to delegate. Begin with administrative tasks and answering the phone, then bookkeeping and clerical, etc. The most successful insurance agent in the country (his name escapes me) set his business up this way. He said, "I learned that I make my money by sitting face to face with prospects—no other way. So I set up my business so that's all I do. I don't make appointments, I don't do bookkeeping and I don't send follow up letters. I get in front of my prospects face to face and sell them insurance. I delegate everything else".

Begin to adopt that mindset and watch your business grow.

Power Days

Sometimes there are days where, for one reason or another, my plate is over flowing and I absolutely must squeeze the most out of every minute. While I don't like working like this all the time, I go into power day mode when necessary.

As a kid growing up on Long Island in the '70's, I was naturally a big fan of the New York Islanders. During their "Dynasty Years" they raised themselves from the worst team in the league to four consecutive world championships. Several times during this incredible run, they found themselves facing elimination from the playoffs. The first time they went down 0-3 in a series, it came out that no team had overcome such a deficit since 1942. They had to win 4 straight games against the very team that had just beaten them three games in a row. The odds were against them.

Sure enough, they pulled it off and won the series. Then they went on to win two more seven game series and another championship.

During one of the post-game interviews the coach was asked how he rallied his team in the face of almost certain elimination. He explained, "I told them that from that (4th) game on, we were going to play the game one line shift at a time. Our goal is to win every single line shift" (for those readers who are not hockey fans, the team puts five new players on the ice at a time—each group is called a line. Each line plays for about one and a half minutes before being replaced by the next line so they can rest and catch their breath).

In other words, he divided the 60 minute game into one and a half minute increments. He told his team we must win each one of these mini (minute and a half) games. By doing so, we'll win the real game. And sure enough, they did.

How does that apply to you? You can divide your day into fifteen minute increments? Then, endeavor to accomplish as much as possible in each fifteen minute section of your day. Don't take unnecessary phone calls, don't allow any interruptions. During each fifteen minute section, stay focused and on track. You will accomplish a great deal.

As I said, I like to limit the number of power days I engage in because they can be pretty intense. Doing them too often leads me to burnout and with my travel schedule I have enough to combat. So be discriminating in your use of Power Days and make the most out of them.

Take Action

Complete the exercise outlined above. Start by listing the 7-10 most important categories in your life. Then Break down each into time frames: 10 years, 5 years, 3 years, 1 year, quarters, this week and today.

Put yourself into a quiet place where you can relax without interruption. Make a list of all goals in each category broken down by time frame. Let your mind soar.

You can do the entire process in a weekend.

Resources

Programs

John Di Lemme- Findyourwhy.com

Tape Sets

Goal Setting by Mike Matzaratta

Time Management by Brian Tracy

Books

The DNA of Success by Jack M. Zufelt

Auto Biography of Mary Kaye Ash

Winning Through Intimidation by Robert J. Ringer

System

RPM System by Tony Robbins.

:01
One Minute Review
Effective Time Management

1. Develop a set of well thought out, written goals and prioritize them.

2. Clearly understand your purpose of each goal.

3. Set out to accomplish each goal in order. Don't be sidetracked by the little things.

4. Plan out each day's activities at the conclusion of the prior day so your sub-conscious can work on it overnight.

chapter 9

Step 8: Get It in Writing

Business Agreements

If you are doing business with other people, you must use written agreements—period. If they are not in writing, you may think you don't have an agreement. That's not true. You do have an agreement, but its terms may be decidedly different from what you thought they were. And it might be some judge or jury who is given the task of figuring out what the agreement was. Usually this happens at the worst possible time; after the fact when emotions have already taken over and every delay or turn of events costs you serious money.

Most business people think of agreements as a means of holding the other party accountable, much as the quote above implies. Yet, there is another, more important purpose than that.

When I practiced law, from time to time, I would prepare business agreements for clients. My client and I would meet in private first and I would take some time to understand the nature of the business and the relationship of my client with his/her potential partner as well as the major concerns and goals of my client.

I might prepare the first draft of the agreement and submit it to the other attorney for review. Shortly thereafter, we would have a four way "sit down" conference where we would negotiate the final terms.

Somewhere along the line, my client would often express a desire to have the upper hand in the business relationship. It would sound something like this: "I want to make sure that he does "X" otherwise it's going to cost him big time. You make sure he suffers if he doesn't do what he says he will - I want to be able to take him to the cleaners."

I understand that sentiment, and there is a place for it in some agreements (Business buy/sells for example). This is a situation where typically there is little on-going interaction between the parties once the deal is consummated. So long as the buyer makes his note payments on time, there is little for he and the seller to discuss after the closing. In most business agreements, inflicting pain should not be anywhere near the top of your list of goals.

In situations where you and your partner are starting or expanding your business relationship, there is a more important purpose for having a written agreement. And that is to understand, clarify and discuss every important aspect of the business relationship so that you can develop a true understanding of your respective needs and expectations.

Sounds a little like Casper Milquetoast. I've been involved in hundreds, perhaps thousands of business agreements; negotiating, drafting, structuring— every aspect imaginable. It has been my experience that the overwhelming reason that business relationships fail is due to poor communication (the business itself may succeed or fail for other reasons). An effective business relationship is all about good communication, and the business relationship for partners is set forth in the written agreement.

Kim, Werner and Andrew were involved in the local real estate investment club. Each had a strong desire to be a real estate investor, yet each felt that alone, s/he was missing some of the necessary tools or resources. They needed the additional support and structure that a partnership can offer, so they decided to "partner up".

They scheduled their first partnership meeting Tuesday evening at Werner's house and outlined their agenda. I was asked to join them to help structure things. The first item on the agenda was choosing a name for the partnership.

Each of the partners had given the subject some prior thought, and Werner shared his first idea. After brief consideration, Kim suggested one of her ideas which also met with resistance.

During the next 45 minutes, the "partners" became more animated in promoting their suggested name and shooting down the other person's idea. Werner and Kim even got nasty with one another and began calling each other "stubborn" and "close minded". Within one hour, the partnership was over because the parties couldn't even select a name.

In truth, it had nothing to do with the name. It had everything to do with control and team work. It was a blessing that they decided not to work together, because if they couldn't even work together to select a name, you can imagine what would happen if a real problem occurred.

Incidentally, no partnership agreement in the world would have kept these three working together. Although each one was a fine individual, they could not work together as a team.

Dave and Andy went to law school together and found themselves to be kindred spirits. Each had an interest in small business and they often got together to discuss their ideas for the perfect business. Dave felt that it must be recession-proof— a product or service that was needed whether the economy was good or bad.

Andy said it must lend itself to systems, so that the founders would not be trapped in the day to day operations. They agreed that service businesses were easier and less expensive to start up so they leaned in that direction.

Dave's family had been involved in the medical field his whole life. His father ran a medical information systems business and Dave and his brother were in the process of writing a medical management software program. Dave's experience taught him that doctors offices are inundated with paper- most of it coming from the insurance company billing process. Andy decided that that type of business could be easily systematized and the need for medical help was unrelated to the economy. This was a recession-proof industry if ever there was one.

Dave and Andy had identified a need and found a solution to an existing problem. Without further discussion, the friends decided to start a medical billing service for doctors (Note: let me know when this starts sounding familiar to you.)

Dave was working a full-time job. He figured he would keep his job and work the business at night and on the weekends. Andy already had one (struggling) business. His time was more flexible, so Dave figured Andy would use his days to market the business. Besides, Andy's affable personality made him the perfect person to do sales. Dave's fiancé, Patty, had recently graduated from law school and had not yet found employment. Dave felt she would be perfect to handle the daily operations.

Andy had a different perspective. Dave had the contacts in the medical field from his father and other family members who moved in medical circles. His uncle was a respected physician and his brother met with hospitals and medical clinics several times a week. Andy would oversee operations. He had extra room in his office suite and he would help develop systems and maintain customer service. Patty's involvement was a non-issue. He felt she had the ability to do the job and other "worker bees" could always be hired, if necessary.

You are probably beginning to see the problem already. The partners each had a viable vision for the business, yet their visions conflicted with one another.

For about two months, Dave would take the one hour drive from his job to Andy's office two or three nights a week. Saturdays he'd come out the whole day. At Dave's suggestion, Andy spent this time calling on every doctor's office in town; yet without a sales and marketing plan, all he got were rejections.

Patty handled operations for the one customer that was referred to them by a friend of Dave's uncle. Although she was bright, she hated paperwork and before long, the entire operation was a mess.

Two months into the process, the partners called it quits. They were tired, disgruntled and upset with each other. Once the business wound down, they never spoke again. By the way, there are now thousands of companies doing this work successfully and making money. A good business idea poorly executed, created a failed business and destroyed a friendship.

It didn't have to be that way.

A good business partnership starts with a good business agreement and a good business plan. We will discuss business plans in another chapter. Let's focus on the likely outcomes that a thoroughly discussed business agreement would have produced.

Initially, Dave would have told Andy that Dave would keep his full time job and that he felt Andy was the best candidate to handle sales and marketing.

Immediately, Andy would have realized that Dave was not in a position to dedicate his full-time efforts to the venture, nor was he able to contribute any start up capital. The business would have to be self financing or Andy would have to make up the shortfall. The friends could have come up with a game plan to accommodate those facts. For example, Andy could have left more time to generate income from his other business and they could have taken steps to minimize the computer equipment they purchased (Dave was setting things up to handle five active processors, when Patty, the one they had, wasn't kept busy by herself).

Andy would have also discussed the fact that he was not trained at all in sales and marketing. Although his personality might have been right, he had no training or desire to go door to door calling on doctors. At that point, the parties could have explored other options like advertising or more importantly, leveraging the relationships that Dave's family had developed over the years. The one customer they had was secured that way. What could they have done to get five more?

And poor Patty— she was in a no-win situation. Andy came to feel that she was being imposed on him simply because she was available or "unemployable" as Andy came to describe it. And Patty felt trapped because she disliked the work yet felt obligated to help out her fiancé, Dave.

The parties should have discussed this in detail prior to launching the business. These problems would have become apparent beforehand, and Dave and Andy could have talked them through. They would have either found solutions or decided not to go into business and preserve the friendship.

You can see that this is not a matter of holding someone's "feet to the fire" or keeping them accountable. All of that is secondary. It is a matter of discovering— uncovering, what each of the parties really wants and seeing if there is a good fit based on reality, not wishes.

A well thought out partnership agreement can take several months to complete. If there is a fatal flaw in the plan or the working relationship, it often shows itself in the first two to four weeks. This is another place that a well trained attorney can be a valuable asset. Their objectivity can help uncover hidden problems much more quickly.

Dave and Andy could have saved themselves a lot of time, money and hardship (not to mention the friendship) if they had invested themselves in a well-drafted agreement.

Still Don't Have an Agreement? Oh Yes You Do!

What happens if you disregard this chapter and nevertheless go into business without a written agreement? Today, most states (if not all) have adopted something called the Uniform Partnership Act (U.P.A.). The act provides for a statutory agreement in the absence of one negotiated by the parties. In other words, if you don't figure out what's best for your partnership, the state does. And if your written partnership agreement fails to address any important topics, the U.P.A. supplies the terms, as well.

Right about now you're thinking, "Oh, thank goodness! Now I don't have to worry about all that negotiating and clarifying—the State does it for me." Not so fast, millionaire in training, you're missing the point!

There is no way that the State can address all of the terms that are important to you. All they've done is to provide an extremely generalized set of terms; something that applies to everyone. As the lawyers say, "It's boilerplate— just plain vanilla". If you rely on the U.P.A. agreement to govern your business, about the only thing that you are guaranteeing is that everybody involved will be disappointed.

How many lawyers does it take to screw in a light bulb (or prepare an agreement)? One for each partner.

The biggest mistake I see business people make regarding agreements is trying to draft it themselves. I suppose they figure that if they are smart enough to run their business, they are smart enough to prepare an agreement. That's like saying "if

I'm smart enough to spell chicken cordon bleu, then I'm smart enough to prepare it."

One has nothing to do with the other.

And don't think you can just grab some agreement off the web and tailor it to your needs. Legal agreements call for special language, "legalize", and you might draft something that means something entirely different than you intended.

For example:

> ☼ **"Consideration" does not mean fellowship as in "he has a lot of consideration for other people."**

> ☼ **A "Corporate Seal" is not a circus animal.**

> ☼ **To "execute" a contract does not mean to gun it down gang-land style.**

> ☼ **And "liquidated damages" is not a type of alcoholic drink.**

Stick to what you are good at. If you are good at finding real estate deals, then do that. If you are a good cook, then do that. Let the lawyers handle the legal stuff.

That said, there is something that you can do to speed the process and keep the costs down. I suggest that you and your partner(s) make an outline of the important terms of your agreement. Spend some time discussing each term. Determine what you agree on, what you disagree on and what you have no basis for an opinion on. This can give the lawyers a head start and save hours and hours of time negotiating at $150 an hour.

Here are some essential terms to include:

- Purpose and scope of the business
- Intended growth
- Roles of the Parties— Who is responsible for what?
- How will the business be capitalized?
- What if additional capital is needed?
- Respective Authority of the parties
- Exclusivity
- Compensation and Division of Profits
- Termination and Dissolution (More on this later)

You may use these as a starting point. Take the first one and discuss it fully. Take notes. See where you agree and disagree. What points did your partner bring up that you hadn't yet thought of? It's not a competition; it's an opportunity to gain clarity and understanding.

Take the first term: purpose and scope of the business. Suppose you intend to invest in real estate. Here are a few things to consider.

Are you buying at foreclosure auction or tax deed auction? What about pre-foreclosure or REO properties? What about buying "subject-to"? Will you fix them up or sell them "as-is"? Do you intend to rent them or flip them? Will you remain in your area (town, county) or travel outside your area? If so, how far? How many deals do you want to do per month? Per year? And so on.

Now, repeat the process for each point listed above and any other points that you feel are important.

It may take several sessions to accomplish this. Once you do, you will have a detailed set of notes to bring to the attorney who will prepare the initial draft.

After discussing your notes, your attorney may suggest several additional points for you and your partner to consider. Now it's time to prepare the first draft.

Drafting the Agreement

The next biggest mistake I see business people make concerning the agreement is only using one attorney to represent both (all) parties. The problem is that although drafting the agreement may not be adversarial, there are still inherent conflicts. Ancient scripture says that no one can serve two masters and no attorney can objectively represent two parties. Don't even put them in that position.

Each party should have his own lawyer. Let one of the lawyers prepare the first draft of the agreement, based on the notes you took during your meetings. She typically will meet with her client and confirm that she has covered everything contained in the client's notes. Then, she will forward it to the other attorney for his review.

Each attorney will have an opportunity to discuss the agreement in private with her client and clarify any uncertainties. When the process is handled this way, there should be relatively few modifications needed. You can each sign off on the agreement and get to the business at hand.

Famous Last Words:
We Don't Need an Agreement, We're Family.

These are right up there with, "There's nothing to worry about, this ship (the Titanic) is unsinkable" and "Honey, let's relax tonight, there's a play over at the Ford theatre. It'll be fun to get out."

Every business needs written agreements, even family businesses. Again, the purpose of the agreement is not to ensure performance or garner trust. You can't do that. It's to clarify issues and avoid misunderstandings. And family businesses are not immune to misunderstandings.

I have come to believe that the most important clauses in a business agreement are the termination clauses. In other words, what happens if we decide to stop working together? Who gets what? How do they get it? What can they do with it? It is far better to think these issues through beforehand, rather than dealing with them in the heat of the moment.

Business termination clauses can take effect under several circumstances: Voluntary Dissolution, Involuntary Dissolution, Death, or Disability. Your agreement should spell out what happens in the event of each of these.

a. **Voluntary Dissolution: This can be the simplest way to end a business relationship. It happens when two people decide to stop working together. Perhaps one partner wants to pursue another venture, or just does not like being in this particular business. Alternatively, it can be a bit heated if the reason for the breakup is voluntary, yet not amicable.**

b. **Involuntary Dissolution: occurs when one partner (or, in the case of a bankruptcy, the trustee or a creditor) decides they want the business to end whether you want to or not.**

c. **Death: The cause is obvious. What is less apparent is that if your partner dies and you are not properly prepared, you can find yourself in business with their well meaning but less agreeable spouse.**

d. **Disability: Illness and injury can prevent one partner from going forward with their responsibilities. The agreement should set forth whether the disabled partner still gets paid, how much and for how long. For example, if a partner becomes ill, you might agree to pay them 100% for 3 months, 50% for 6 more months and buy them out if they are unable to return to full time work after 9 months.**

Having considered the possible circumstances leading to the termination, you must now consider some details for each one:

a. **Valuation: You should agree, in advance, to a method of valuing the business and therefore, each parties share of it. The value of the business will change over time, so it is important to specify a means of updating that value.**

b. **Terms of the Buyout: Is the purchase price due up front or are payments acceptable? How much, how often? What does the departing partner need? What can the remaining partner afford to pay?**

c. **Funding the Buyout: Some business people purchase insurance to fund the buyout. In the example of a partner dying, a life insurance policy would cover the cost of the buyout. Again the value of the policy must be carefully considered so that there are sufficient proceeds to pay for the buyout.**

As you can see, there are many things to consider regarding the termination of your business relationship. This preparatory work will pay off in spades.

Kate and Johnny

Kate and Johnny were experienced restaurant owners, having had interests in several different restaurants over the years. Johnny was an excellent cook; Kate is great with people and knew how to run the front end. They had recently located to a place that was badly in need of great Italian food, yet, neither of them wanted to work the long hours that their prior businesses required.

Cousin George had also recently moved to the area and was interested in starting a new business. Although he had never owned a restaurant before, he was a successful businessman and felt he could "run the operation". He also had the needed capital to complete the deal.

So, they decided to start a restaurant from scratch. The new shopping center in town was the perfect location and they could design and build out the space exactly the way they wanted. With all the new homes being built in the area, there would be plenty of people to feed. They shook hands on it and agreed—we don't need a written agreement, we're family. Everyone got to work.

The next four months they were busy working with landlords and architects, pulling building permits and working with inspectors. Everything came together, pretty much as planned and in September the restaurant opened. The grand opening was a success and they got busy "working out the bugs". All was well with the world.

Then, just two weeks into their successful little enterprise, George dropped a bomb. He called his partner aside and said "Johnny, I hate the restaurant business." Johnny looked puzzled. After all, everything had been going so well. George went on,

"I've been chained to that front counter for two weeks, and I'm going nuts. I'm not used to being in one place all day long. I like to be out meeting with people on job sites, taking in the sun and fresh air. The smell of pizza is starting to make me sick. I gotta get out of here!"

Johnny couldn't believe what he was hearing. What's not to like? Business has been great. The customers are all great people. We've got a goldmine here. What's George talking about? "George, maybe you just need to get away for the weekend. We've all been working hard launching the business. Take a few days to relax and you'll feel different on Monday."

Unfortunately, things hadn't changed by Monday. In fact, George was more sure than ever that he wanted out of the business. "Now, Johnny," he said. "You've got to buy me out right away!"

The nightmare had begun.

Johnny was stunned. He and Kate had invested their life savings in the place. How could they buy George out? More importantly, the reason Johnny needed a partner in the business was because he had some health challenges a couple of years prior. He knew he couldn't take the physical demands of running the restaurant alone with Kate. Suddenly, his life savings was at risk and his future was unraveling.

He convinced George to give him a couple of months to figure out a plan, and George agreed to hang in there temporarily.

Over the ensuing weeks, it became clear that although George wanted out of the business, he still wanted to manage it— in his own way. This put everyone at odds. Before long, the employees didn't know who to listen to and George started getting loud in front of the customers. George started closing early, without consulting with his partners. He would fire staff and then not show up for his shift.

Then, he had a change of heart. He decided that he liked the business; it was Kate and Johnny that he didn't like. He continued to create havoc, changing the menu, refusing to pay for supplies and undermining the authority of Kate and Johnny with the staff. He took the business check book and refused to report the restaurants' receipts from his shift. He went to the bank and attempted to have Kate and Johnny removed from the checking account. There was no way to win.

Kate and Johnny saw their life savings going down the drain and they felt powerless to doing anything about it. Finally, they went to an attorney who felt he could negotiate a settlement. After trying for over two months to work something out, the lawyer brought them the bad news. It was time to cut their losses and start a lawsuit. George was not willing to reason with anyone. Their only hope was to get a court order to sell the business and recoup whatever they could. Otherwise they stood to lose everything. Oh, by the way, the lawsuit will cost $5,000 - $10,000 in legal fees if everything goes well, and no, the judge won't make George pay for it.

They were devastated. This started out as a friendly and successful business. Now it's World War III.

This is real life, folks. Partners don't start out unruly, but people do crazy things when under pressure. Crazy actions lead to crazy responses and before long you've got an all out battle on your hands.

The next six months were misery for Kate and Johnny. It was like being on a runaway train. The business was being destroyed but their hands were tied. Anything they did to correct a problem was undone by George. They were exhausted, financially strapped and were just about at their breaking point.

For some unknown reason, George had another change of heart. His lawyer said that he had decided to sell the business (Thankfully, Kate and Johnny had prepared for this by securing a loan). After several weeks of roller coaster negotiations, they bought George out and restored the restaurant to order.

The tragedy is that all of this could have been avoided with a simple agreement. The termination clause could have said, "If one of the parties wants out of the business, this is what happens. They will be paid so much, over this amount of time, etc, etc." It would have been quick, orderly, and a lot less costly—emotionally and financially.

The choice is yours. You can pay the attorneys a couple of thousand dollars to prepare a written partnership agreement or you can pay them tens of thousands to fight it out in court.

Take Action

1. Sit down with your partner(s)-to-be and review the clauses above. Discuss them, consider the alternatives and decide how you want your business to be run.

2. Take thorough notes and prepare an outline. Review your outline with your business attorney and have her prepare the first draft.

3. Complete the process and put the agreement to bed.

4. Get to the business of doing business.

Resources

Bar Association

Call your local Bar Association for a referral to a capable business attorney.

:01
One Minute Review
Get it in Writing

1. Business Agreements should be used to clarify roles and positions, not impose ones will .

2. If you don't put your agreement in writing, the law will do it for you.

3. Don't prepare your own legal agreements. Get the assistance of effective legal counsel.

4. The negotiation process serves many useful purposes. Don't try to rush things along.

chapter 10

Step 9: Building Relationships

Early in their legal careers, Andy and Trish took on virtually any new client they could get. After all, money was tight and there were bills to pay. Trish handled the litigation for the firm, Andy had business interests.

Anxious to start generating income, Trish often took on cases before receiving the full retainer. One case called for $1,500 up front billed against $150 per hour. Yet, the client only had $500 at that moment. Trish agreed to handle the case for $500 up front, so long as the client gave her the $1,000 balance at the first court appearance. Another case called for $2,500 up front. This client only had $1250, so Trish made her the same deal.

The first case was more work than Trish had expected. Between legal briefs, discovery and depositions, she had 15 hours of preparation time in on the case prior to the first court date. No problem, she reasoned, the client will pay me when we get to court. She even sent a letter to the client detailing the hours she had already invested, expecting that would give him the chance to make the necessary arrangements.

On court day, the client showed up looking very concerned. He ran over to Trish and started rambling on and on about his case and how unfairly he was being treated, and how much stress the case was putting on him. This isn't a good time to discuss money, Trish thought, I'll wait till after we see the judge.

After Trish argued her client's case, the judge rendered a decision mostly in the client's favor. The fines would be minimal, with some small court costs. Once the legal fees were paid, the client would get through the experience virtually unscathed. The client shook Trish's hand, thanked her profusely and started to leave the courthouse. "Wait!" Trish said, "what about the money you owe me?"

"Oh, I'll send you a check when I can. Thanks again for your help."

 A week later, no check; two weeks later, still nothing. Not even a returned phone call. After a month, Trish got angry and decided to sue the client for the money she was rightfully owed.

In the meantime, something similar happened with the second client. The installment plan was not honored and she stopped returning Trish's calls as well. She decided to sue the second client as well.

During the first 6 months of her practice, ten clients failed to pay Trish as agreed. In fact, she had as many non-paying clients as paying clients. "The heck with it." she said, "I'll just sue all of them at once!"

Meanwhile, Andy wasn't doing too much better in the business relationship department. During this time, he had been busy putting together several business deals. The first one was a small residential housing development involving the construction of ten single family homes. Andy was banking on this project to get his new business off the ground. Unfortunately, the market had turned and the project started to unravel. After a year of preparation, the investment partners decided that this was not a good time to move forward.

More than disappointed, Andy saw this as a serious financial blow to him personally. He felt that the investors had "set him up" and wasted a great deal of his time. He vowed never to do business with them again.

Instead, he turned his attention to another project his partner Jim had been putting together. He and Jim had been close friends since college and they enjoyed the excitement of working on deals together. This one was particularly complicated. It involved arbitrage; a new concept to them both. The deal had been brought to them by another mutual friend, Dave, who had connections with all the "right people". Dave had been working in the New York financial center for one of the biggest institutions in the world. He assured Jim and Andy that everything was in order. In fact, he told them that the deal would bring them $100,000 in profit in less than six months. "I've done my due diligence", he vowed.

Andy and Jim decided to put the necessary $30,000 into the deal. It wasn't all the money they had, but it meant committing all of their available investment capital. "It's just for six months", they agreed. "Then we'll put half of the profit into a reserve fund."

About two months later, Jim called Andy into his office. "We have a problem," he explained. "The deal went bad. Our $30,000 investment was stolen along with another $1 million that belonged to other investors. The F.B.I. is involved and the whole thing is a mess." Ultimately, at least one person went to federal prison over the matter.

"What about Dave's due diligence?" Andy yelled. "I thought he had checked everything about this deal out? And you, Jim, you're responsible, too. What are you going to do to get our $30,000 back? Tell Dave and the rest of those jokers that there will be a lawsuit! Heads will roll over this one!"

Within a week, Dave and Andy had become adversaries. The friendship between Andy and Jim had taken a beating and within two months, the friends were no longer speaking. The partnership broke up and they went their separate ways.

And so it went. In about a year's time, Trish and Andy were left standing in a pile of ashes. The trail of carnage left in their wake was staggering and they were left wondering how anyone can survive in this dog eat dog world of business.

It doesn't have to be this way. Remember: Business is not about the deals, it's about the relationships.

Turn the Tables - Add Value First

One of my good friends, best selling author of the book *Conversations With Millionaires*, Mike Litman teaches a powerful technique that can greatly improve your success and add hundreds of thousands of dollars to your income over time. It's simply this: in every business conversation that you have, ask the other party this question, "What can I do to help you?" It's a simple question with profound impact.

Let me explain. The first time I spoke with Mike, he had called me to review several tax strategies that he could implement himself. His book had just become a best seller and his income had jumped significantly. "I've got a problem and I need your help", he said. "I just made a lot of money from my book." "So, what's the problem?" I asked. (It didn't sound like a problem to me). "My accountant told me I am going to get killed with taxes," he sighed. I said, "Let's talk about a few things that should be helpful." and we spent the next fifteen minutes discussing three strategies that saved him tens of thousands of dollars.

Mike was very appreciative and before we hung up with each other, he asked me about some of the projects I was working on. I told him about an important one involving internet marketing and his next question changed our relationship forever. He asked, "How can I help you with that?" Surprised, I replied, "I don't know.... Do you know anyone who is an expert in internet marketing?" "Yes", he said. "Would you like me to call him and introduce the two of you?" "Wow! I'd really appreciate that." My project took a leap forward and a new friendship was born.

Since that time, virtually every time we speak, Mike asks me if there is anything he can do to help me. And now I do the same. We have become good friends and valuable resources to one another.

Take It to the Next Level: The Laurie Wong Exercise

About a year ago, I received phone calls from several business associates concerning a project they were considering getting involved in. Its called "Kids on Target", they said. Laurie Wong from Atlanta Georgia designed it as a way to teach teenagers the secrets of financial freedom. After all, isn't it better to teach kids at that age how to do it properly, rather than wait until they've gotten themselves all twisted up financially and then intervene?

The program has a number of components, but one set is particularly interesting. It's a three year program for kids in 6th grade, 7th grade and 8th grade. As six graders, the kids are taught, "hands on" the basics of business and given the opportunity to start and manage their own business. As a class they chose a business to go into and then they are broken down into small groups to manage the various business departments. The first year, Laurie's kids chose to start a snack bar at their school. "There was no cafeteria, and no other way for the students to get something to eat or drink during the day", they reasoned.

Laurie assigned a few students to handle inventory and a few others to handle sales. Two kids were in charge of running the cash register and two different students ran the bookkeeping. The sales department designed flyers which they distributed into the student's lockers each day. A different snack or drink combination was featured each day.

The students voted that if their business made enough money, they would go on a Disney cruise at the end of the school year.

In June, they calculated their net profits and discovered that they had made about $60,000—more than enough for their cruise. They had a wonderful sense of accomplishment.

The next year, Laurie had the returning business kids (now 7th graders) teach what they had learned to the new 6th graders. They developed systems and learned to supervise the younger kids while they worked to grow the business. Another successful year led to another cruise—at their choice.

In the third year, Laurie taught the children to tithe or give back to the community. They decided themselves which charity to support and at the end of another successful year, they proudly presented a donation check to a local church. They were incredibly proud of themselves.

When I heard about Laurie and her "Kids on Target" program, I welcomed the opportunity to fly to Atlanta and meet her, along with my business associates. Laurie had pre-arranged to use a small conference room to present her concept to all five of us at once.

As she introduced herself, she positioned herself near the "white board" at the front of the room. She started by writing the names of each participant on it: Drew, Matt, Mike, Kathy and Bryan. Then she observed that, "We have three hours together today, so that gives us 30 minutes per person." I'm thinking **30 minutes for what**? She explained, "I'd like each of you to take a few minutes and write down your #1 goal for the year. What is the single most important thing for you to accomplish this year? Please write it down."

Then, she asked each of us what our goal was and she wrote it down under each of our names on the white board. She started with me and after writing down my goal; she turned to the other folks in the room and asked, "Can anyone do anything to help Drew reach his goal?" Mike stepped in and offered to introduce me to several people that could help out. Next, Matt did the same thing. Kathy had two suggestions for me and Bryan shared a few resources himself. And of course, Laurie had three people she knew of who could assist me.

This went on for almost 30 minutes, with Laurie facilitating the process with each of the participants offering resources and assistance. Bottom line: by the time they were done with me, there was no way that I couldn't achieve my goal. I was floored.

I had flown into town under the auspices of helping Laurie out and she had found a way to help me more than I could ever help her.

Then she repeated the process with each of the other participants. Each one of us was in a far better position because of that meeting than before we had arrived.

By the time she was finished, she had significantly benefited all five of us. She spent the last half hour describing her program and requesting our financial support. How could we say no? We gladly supported her program and made lasting friendships.

Here are some practical suggestions you can incorporate into your daily business life:

1) View people as lifetime customers

It's easy in a retail or service business to see customers on a transaction by transaction basis. After all, they come into our store to buy a dozen eggs and when they leave, we have no way of knowing if we'll ever see them again. As a result, we're inclined to treat them that way, perhaps with a little less TLC than if we knew they'll be back in a few days. And we train our employees the same way.

Instead, try treating each customer as if you expect to see them every few days for the rest of your life. Look at their initial contact as an opportunity to establish a long term relationship (even if they don't purchase anything).

Answer their questions cheerfully. Address their concerns

promptly. Handle their problems as if they are your friends.

You'll set into motion an entirely different type of relationship. If you are providing a needed product or service at a fair price and you treat them like valued friends, you will have a customer for life. And, if twenty-five percent of your revenue goes back toward bringing in new customers, your cost of doing business will drop dramatically. You'll have an ongoing source of newly referred customers and your business will grow successfully.

2) Be fair. Treat others the way you would like to be treated in similar circumstances.

I didn't invent this one. It was written in the Bible thousands of years ago and it remains just as true today.

I know some business people that go to such lengths to protect themselves and their business interests, that they unnecessarily hurt their customers in the process. Perhaps they've been hurt in business themselves, and they've become paranoid. They practically view their customers and business associates as the enemy.

It can be seen in their return policy. "No refunds, No returns, no matter what." It keeps the number of returns down, but it kills the chance to build a relationship.

Or, they'll run a "Special of the week" and if a customer calls to order it a day late, they refuse to extend the offer.

You don't have to give the store away, just extend yourself a little and be fair.

3) Use disagreements as an opportunity to gain understanding

Early in my career, I was a scrappy New Yorker. My training ground was the football field and the hockey rink. If I didn't like the way something was going, I got loud and nasty. It came with the territory. In business, I damaged a lot of important business relationships.

Those rules don't work in business.

These days, I have far fewer disputes. But, I've learned that when the occasional dispute arises, it can be used as an opportunity to build the relationship. As Steven Covey teaches—seek first to understand, then to be understood. Give others the space to have their own opinion and perspective, even if it differs from yours.

4) Clarify your expectations—put them in writing

We already covered this in detail in the chapter on Written Agreements. Remember the old adage an ounce of prevention is worth a pound of cure? It applies here. Well thought out written agreements will uncover your expectations and clarify them for yourself and your partners. This saves time and money and preserves relationships.

5) Take responsibility and make the needed adjustments

There is one certainty in business—things will go wrong. It's an inherent part of the process. The key is to take responsibility for the mistakes that get made and the problems that occur and fix them. Responsibility doesn't mean feeling bad about it or blaming your partners or employees. It means recognizing that because you have a stake in the situation, you have an obligation to solve the problem. It doesn't matter whose fault it was. That's a loser's line of questioning.

Winners seek to identify the cause of the problem as well as several possible solutions. How could the problem have been avoided? What did you do to contribute to it? Then, agree on a new course of conduct and move on. Be ready to make further adjustments. It's not the problems that cause businesses to succeed or fail. It's your response to those problems.

Take responsibility and course correct. That's a winner's approach.

6) Promise less, Deliver more

If there is one thing that can catapult your business into success it's this: always deliver more than you promise. Some business people feel that they have to promise the moon in order to get the customer in the first place and that there's nothing left to give customers to ensure their satisfaction. It's just not true. There is always more to give.

Here are a few examples:

a. **Bonus program (free report or audio) that better explains what they purchased or teaches the customer to get more benefit out of it. For example, if you sell a piece of furniture, you could add a special report on how to clean it or stain proof it.**

b. **A free telephone coaching session.**

c. **A discount on their next purchase from you.**

d. **A discount for using a preferred vendor. For example,**

when I practiced law, I gave our real estate clients a dis-count voucher for a local moving company or restaurant.

e. A bonus CD about another program of interest that you offer.

f. A free yearly update and analysis.

The list is endless. The point is you want to give the customer more than they anticipated. The extra bonus will let them know that you value their business and the information will keep them connected to your business.

Enlarge the Pie Before Dividing It

Inevitably, when negotiating a new deal or in the course of business itself, the time will come when you have to agree on the division of the spoils. Should you split the profits 50/50, 90/10 or somewhere in the middle? I'll share a couple of tips that I find helpful.

In my early days in business, I was intent on getting the best deal I could for myself. After all, if I didn't take care of me, who would? While I still recognize the importance of structuring a great deal for myself, I have learned that the deal must be worthwhile for my partner or business associates.

One thing I do now is to make sure that there is enough left on the table to make the deal viable for everyone involved. Otherwise, someone may be forced to do a particular deal, but we'll never have a lasting business relationship. It's called win/win negotiating and it means that in order to structure a lasting deal, everyone must have a victory. No one gets taken advantage of.

The philosophy is based on the knowledge that you'll have a much more successful and satisfying business career if you develop a core group of business associates and partners you can continue to do business with instead of burning through relationships after taking advantage of people.

I've found an approach that works better for me: Enlarge the pie first then divide it more favorably to everyone. In other words, find as many ways as possible to sweeten the pot. Find out what else can benefit your partners. Make the pie bigger first, before dividing it. Then everyone gets more pie than expected.

Often, it costs you nothing to make the deal better for your partners. For example, you may introduce a partner to someone who he can do another deal with. Or, you may have a resource available to help them with a marketing or supply problem. Add those things into the deal. Your partners benefit, it won't cost you anything, and it turns a good deal into a great deal.

Stay in Touch Diary

One last thing about building relationships is the importance of staying in consistent touch. You can do it with a 'Stay in Touch Diary". The premise of the diary is that the more business you do with someone, the more frequent the contact needs to be. Yet, there are some people that may be useful resources at some point, even though you're not working on a deal with them currently.

Set up a table like this:

Stay in Touch Diary	
Daily	
✓	Mari
✓	Linda
✓	Mike

Weekly	
✓	Ted
✓	Mark D
✓	Laurie
✓	Mark B
Biweekly	
✓	Patricia
✓	Barry
✓	Gabby
Monthly	
✓	Al
Quarterly	
✓	Herman
✓	Kath
✓	Greg
Semi-Annually	
✓	Mike
✓	Brian

A five minute check-in call can go a long way. You can say, "It's my monthly check-in call and I just wanted to see if there is anything I can do to support you." An occasional card or hand written note will be particularly memorable—it's much better than an email. Just "✓" off the people you've made contact with and update your list regularly.

Take Action

1. Start doing business ONLY with people you admire and respect.

2. Commit to doing win-win deals. Start asking your business associates how you can help them with a project or deal they're working on.

3. Call 3 people this week and ask, "What is your most important goal this month? How can I help you achieve it?"

Resources

Books

The DNA of Relationships by Gary Smalley, M.D.

How to Win Friends and Influence People by Dale Carnegie

How to Think Bigger Than You Ever Thought You Could Think by Mark Victor Hanson

---

:01
One Minute Review
Business Relationships

---

1. Enter business relationships slowly and treat them with respect.

2. Seek to add value before dividing the pie.

3. View your customers and prospects as lifetime relationships.

4. Under promise and over deliver.

5. Stay in regular touch with business associates, even when there are no hot deals pending.

chapter 11

Step 10: You've Gotta Have a Plan

> I find it fascinating that most people plan their
> vacations with better care than they do their lives.
> Perhaps that is because escape is easier than change.
> -Jim Rohn

In order to succeed at anything you've got to have a plan. Business is no different. Yet, depending on the type of business you're operating, the plan will vary.

For example, if you are raising money from investors or bringing a company public, you need a lengthy and comprehensive plan. It must not only provide a realistic strategy for running the business successfully, but it must also demonstrate to potential investors your knowledge of the business and your ability to foresee problems and solve them. A good plan will also include comprehensive market research and your response to it, and a detailed proforma that shows worst case, best case and most likely financial projections over a three to five year period. It takes three to five months to put a comprehensive business plan together.

These days it's much easier to put together a "canned" business plan. Just buy one of a hundred "fill in the blanks" software applications or download the forms from the web and tailor it to your needs. In an hour or so you'll have a 40 or 50 page professional looking business plan with financial projections and color coded diagrams. The problem is that your professional looking plan will be almost useless.

Most of the information will be provided by the software program, not your thorough research. Yet it's the research that gives you your "feel" for the business; your knowledge of the business inside and out. It's not how fancy your business plan looks that will determine the success of your business; it's your true knowledge of the industry and its needs and your ability to respond to those needs.

Let's Get Practical

I suggest that you put together a one or two page plan; actually more of an outline. It will cover the most important components of your business and give you the steps needed to launch your business or take it to the next level during the next twelve months. The components will vary depending on the type of business you are operating, but the core ideas will be similar.

For example, let's say Kelly and Wally have decided to start their own restaurant. Wally has worked as a primary cook for over 15 years mostly for small family owned Italian restaurants. Kelly has been in the restaurant business for 12 years, waiting tables and managing front room operations.

After giving it a lot of thought, they've decided to start their own place. They each feel strongly that they can handle the day to day management; they've been doing it for other people for over a decade each.

The part that's new to them is what they call the "ownership stuff"—finding a location; signing a lease, handling the finances – bookkeeping and accounting and bringing in the business.

They have decided to work with two mentors: Chris and Tony. Tony has worked in his family restaurant for over twenty years, since he was twelve years old. As his parents got older, he took over all operations and has run the business very successfully; adding a second location seven years ago and a third location three years ago.

Chris has started and successfully run three different businesses, a retail shop and a marketing firm. He is also a successful real estate investor; owning five commercial buildings in the area.

They've been laying the ground work for the last four months and feel pretty sure they can have everything in place in about three months.

Here's a sample plan for their new restaurant.

1. **Name of Business: Cousins Pizza and Pasta**

2. **Nature of Business: Italian Restaurant and Pizza Kitchen. Family restaurant (wine and beer only) open daily for lunch and dinner**

3. **Personnel:**

   🕐 **Management: Kelly and Wally**

   🕐 **Roles:**
   - **Wally - menu design, cooking, managing kitchen**
   - **Kelly - dining room design and management, dining room staff hiring, training, management**

🕒 **Staff:**

(2) Servers

(1) Assistant cook/kitchen help

4. Operations:

🕒 Wally arrives at 9 am for noon openings to check food delivery and prepare food for the day. Wally takes a break from 3 to 5 and returns for dinner crowd

🕒 Kelly arrives at 11 to prep and train staff on daily specials, etc. Last seating is 8:30

🕒 Kelly and Wally close with staff from 9-10

🕒 We'll give ourselves a few months to work out the kinks and start to market the business more diligently after that

5.   Marketing:

a. Grand Opening May 1st - Newspaper ads, invite local business people and politicians.

b. Display ads in local paper - Coupons for "special of the week"

c. "Business Flyer" ad on local Cable station

d. Distribute flyers to local homeowners, apartment houses and office buildings

e. 25% off Lunch and Dinner specials on slow days (Mon. and Tues.)

6. Financial:

Investment: $100,000

Goal Recoup investment within 5 years

	Sales	Recoup
Months 1-3	$4,000	$0
Months 4-6	$6,000	$500
Months 7-12	$8,000	$1,000
Months 13-24	$10,000	$1,500
Months 25-36	$12,000	$2,000
Months 36-48	$13,000	$2,500
Months 49-60	$14,000	$3,000

7. **Ultimate Vision:** To have two locations fully staffed and systematized so Kelly and I can manage and supervise them without having to do operations work.

8. **Mentoring:** We will meet with Chris on the first Thursday of each month and with Tony every Tuesday morning over a cup of coffee.

9. **Tithing:** Once the business is financially viable (6 consecutive profitable months) we'll set up a tithing account for St. Jude's hospital for children. Initially we'll deposit five percent of net profits and increase it from there.

Steps to Accomplish: 3 Months to Grand Opening

Month 1:

1. Confirm Capital - savings, Uncle Lou

2. Research location and competition

3. Decide on Location; sign lease

4. Set up corporation

Month 2:

1. Order tables, chairs and equipment

2. Contact suppliers re. food, beverages, wine and beer

3. Get wine and beer license

4. Prep initial menu

Month 3:

1. Finalize menu

2. Hire/train staff

3. Place ads; announce Grand opening

The plan Kelly and Wally put together provides a good road map for launching their business. It's an overview of the "big picture" combining what they knew when they started the R&D phase of their business along with their reasonable expectations for the future.

Let's see how things played out for Kelly and Wally (our first plan).

They caught a break finding a location. A nearby shopping center was doing so well that it was expanding so it had room for 5 more stores. One of them was slated to be a sandwich shop, but the owner had a falling out with his partner, so they decided not to go into business. The permits were in place and some of the preliminary construction was already complete, so Kelly and Wally got a head start.

Uncle Lou had committed to $60,000 in start up capital; the rest would have to come from savings. But when the time came to write the check, Uncle Lou could only come up with half of what he had promised. After recovering from the initial shock and disappointment, Kelly and Wally decided to take a home equity loan out against their home. It was a little unsettling at first because they realized that if the business failed, they could lose their home as well. But after weighing things out, they decided to take out the loan and agreed between themselves to pay off the equity line first, prior to repaying Uncle Lou or replacing their savings.

The equipment, food, tables and chairs were easy to locate; Kelly and Wally had been doing business with the suppliers for years. There was one snag with the pizza oven—the model Wally wanted was on back order. The delay forced them to move the grand opening back two weeks.

The menu came together easily. The most difficult part was deciding which dishes would make the final cut. They agreed that some of their personal favorites would be added into later menus or offered as weekly specials.

Opening Day was a huge success from a marketing perspective. They had more customers than they could handle. They were overwhelmed with customers and had over an hour wait for a table. They recovered well from that because Kelly offered them a free glass of wine to thank them for being patient. All and all everyone was happy.

Tragedy seemed to strike when a waitress quit the first week during a busy shift and then the assistant cook walked out two days later. They had to scramble to cover the shortfall, but they were able to hire and train replacements.

They continued to meet with Chris and Tony who helped them course correct as things unfolded. Having experienced mentors proved to be a lifesaver. It smoothed out much of the emotional ups and downs and allowed them to find quicker solutions to their problems.

Which leads to the next point: Step 10 - The Rule is You've Gotta Have a Plan.

But the corollary to Step 10 is: Things never go according to plan!

It's a Road Map

A business plan is no different from any other plan. Things happen along the way that may take you off course. The question is how should you respond to the distractions?

Years ago I decided to make a vacation of seeing the beauty of this country by going from national park to national park camping in a tent. Because I was beginning my journey in Long Island, New York, I had little choice other than to head west. A friend of mine who had made a similar trip several years before me spent a few hours reviewing his journey one evening (mentors). I plotted a course that included the most interesting and beautiful places I knew of and laid it all out on a map.

My first stop was to St. Louis to see the arch alongside the Mississippi river; then on to Colorado to see the beauty of Rocky Mountain National Park. On to Garden of the Gods Park, the Grand Canyon along with Bryce and Zion, around to see the Great Salt Lake in Utah, up to Yellowstone and turn the corner to see Mount Rushmore before returning home.

I became a member of AAA (mentors), both for their road side assistance program and for their incredible flip-chart style maps. I bought the needed supplies, got my car checked out by a mechanic, and planned my departure date. Everything was ready.

I figured I'd get a good night's sleep that night and get on the road by 4:30 am to beat the New York commuter traffic. I got to bed early with thoughts of my pending adventure and laid there waiting to fall asleep. And laid there… and laid there…… I was too excited—there was no way I could get myself to sleep. So I got up at 11 p.m., took a quick shower and hit the road four and a half hours early. My trip had barely begun and I was already off plan.

By six a.m. I was very sleepy, so I took a nap in the car at a truck stop just off route 80 in Pennsylvania. I arrived in St. Louis a little earlier than originally anticipated, but fairly close to the plan I had put together. And so it went for the rest of the trip—my carefully crafted plan was more of a road map (literally) than a set of hard and fast rules.

And so it will be with your business plan. There will be detours; some positive, some negative. The key to success is distinguishing between the two types of detours and working through them appropriately.

There's More Than One Right Way

One hint is to be concerned more with the outcome (results) than with the path (method). In other words, if the deviation is simply a different way of producing the same or a better outcome, it's a positive deviation. If the deviation results in missing an important goal or deadline, it's a negative deviation.

This is why building a successful business is more of an art than a science.

Dishonest Partner(s), inconsistent employees and unreliable vendors are all negative deviations. If you find yourself in business with these types of people, you need to make big changes. You cannot build a successful business surrounded with these kinds of people.

Missed goals, surges in orders, running slightly behind schedule, an ad campaign that under-produces—these are all deviations that can be worked around and overcome. You need to evaluate them as part of the "big picture" and decide whether they are heading you down a dead end, or pointing to another path that will get you to a better result.

Here's a technique that will help you to evaluate deviations and help you overcome them:

Have ten backups for each major part of your plan and five backups for the minor parts of the plan!

As a kid, I was enthralled with the Apollo space program. I watched every launch, every moon landing and every moon walk on T.V. During one of the press conferences after the Apollo 11 mission, a reporter asked Neil Armstrong, "Sir, suppose you were sitting there in the Lunar Module about to blast off from the moon and the rocket didn't fire. You've only got 2 hours of oxygen left at that point. What would you do? Would you pray, would you ask to speak to your wife on the radio? How would you spend your last two hours?"

Armstrong answered without hesitation. He said, "I'd spend the two hours fixing the problem." That's the difference between success and failure. Successful people solve problems; unsuccessful people get stopped by them.

Many people now realize that a big part of an astronaut's training is working in flight simulators responding to problems. In fact, those simulators are programmed with every imaginable problem they can encounter and the astronauts are trained to "work the solutions" one at a time until the problem is solved.

Business is no different. You will be faced with problems. A big part of handling them effectively is thinking them through ahead of time and preparing your responses in advance. The more alternative solutions you can develop, the better prepared for setbacks you will be.

Let's take another look at Kelly and Wally's restaurant.

There were several major areas of their initial plan: Personnel, Financial and Marketing. Let's go through each area and brainstorm possible solutions. An important part of brainstorming is to list all possible solutions without passing judgment on any one of them. Just let the ideas flow and organize a plan at the end of the brainstorming session. Often, an idea might seem unusual, even nonsensical at first, but with some refinement it might prove very useful.

I. Personnel: Other than the two slots that Kelly and Wally fill, they need 3 employees: 2 servers and an assistant in the kitchen. If someone fails to show up for a shift, or doesn't work well with the rest of the team, it would be a big problem. Here are some options Kelly and Wally can implement if needed.

> **1. Hire and train an extra crew knowing that some people will drop out**
>
> **2. Let one crew work one day and the other crew work the next day until they prove themselves**
>
> **3. Have a "help wanted" ad ready for the newspaper**
>
> **4. Have a "help wanted" sign ready to hang up in the restaurant window**
>
> **5. Contact 2 temporary help agencies**
>
> **6. Speak to waiters and waitresses at other restaurants in the area about their availability**
>
> **7. Speak to waiters and waitress at other restaurants about their friends**

8. Put a help wanted ad on the local cable T.V.

9. Ask another restaurant owner if they have extra help you can use

10. Ask another restaurant owner if you can share an employee on alternating days

II. **Operating Capital:** Kelly and Wally need $100,000 to launch their business. How can they come up with the money?

1. Savings

2. Borrow from Friends

    a. Jim and Tammy

    b. Bob

    c. Eileen

3. Borrow from family

    a. Uncle Lou

    b. Gabe

    c. Mom

4. Get a bank Loan

5. Home equity Loan

6. Borrow against stock portfolio

7. Owner financing

8. Personal line of Credit

9. Outside Debt financing

10. Bring in a partner

III. **Marketing:** Marketing is ALL about testing, so Kelly and Wally need to be prepared to test, test, test. Their marketing plan already has five components. But, let's suppose for our example that each of the components fails in some way. How can they plan in advance to respond?

   a. Grand Opening May 1st

      i. Extend the grand opening through the following weekend

      ii. Try a different newspaper

      ii. Use a display ad instead of a classified

      iii. Put an insert into the newspaper

      iv. Tell the politicians to bring their staff in for a free meal

      v. Ask the local business people to distribute "one free meal" coupons as a gift to their customers

   b. Display ads in local paper - Coupons for "special of the week"

      i. Change the headline on the ad

      ii. Change the headline again

      iii. Change the location of the ad in the paper

      iv. Try a different newspaper(s)

      v. Get a restaurant review printed

      vi. Advertise "There is such a thing as a free lunch" day

    c. "Business Flyer" ad on local Cable station

        i. Change the headline on the ad

        ii. Change the time of day the ad runs

        iii. Change stations

        iv. Change the copy content

        v. Change the offer

    d. Distribute Flyers to local homeowners, apartment houses and office buildings

        i. Distribute them repeatedly

        ii. Change the copy

        iii. Change the offer

        iv. Distribute more of them (other locations)

    e. 25% off Lunch and Dinner specials on slow days (Mon. and Tues.)

    f. Add\Change offers

        i. Buy 10 Pizzas, get one free

        ii. Buy two full meals get one free

        iii. Bring a friend, they eat free

If you want more confidence and certainty, you can do this process with every area of your business plan. Sit down by yourself or with your partner (or mentor) and brainstorm each issue. The more alternative solutions you have, the better prepared you'll be.

Here is a plan for Christina's internet marketing business. She has been studying internet marketing for about a year, having been to three multi day seminars. This could be a new business or an additional stream of income for an existing business.

Name of Business: Web Marketing Concepts

Nature of Business: Marketing information products and other items on the internet.

Initial Obstacle to Overcome: We have no products to offer

Proposed Solutions: Obtain the rights to sell several products by means of Joint Ventures, Licensing agreements and developing our own products over time.

Required Equipment & Resources: Home Office, Upgraded PC with DSL, Battery Backup, back up hard drive, Web design software, access to web hosting services.

Status: Already in place

Operations: Once the product rights have been secured, I'll develop an on-line "turnkey" system that generates leads, converts sales and takes orders online. My J.V. and licensee partners will do the fulfillment.

Marketing: I'll use a combination of the following:

    a. Build a list of 10,000

    b. E-mails

    c. Teleclasses

    d. Snail mailers

e. Magazine Ads

f. On-line ads

g. Banners

h. Sales letter page

The emails, magazine ads, on-line ads, banners and letters will drive prospects to attend the teleclasses, and the teleclasses will drive prospects to the sales letter page directly.

Financial: The total cost of setting up each product will be $3,000 or less.

I expect to sell products in the $500 range with a 50/50 split or $250 per sale.

My goal is to sell one product a week during the first 2 months after launch, then 3 products a week for the next 3 months, building to 1 product per day within the first year.

Tentative Launch Date: May 1st

Revenue per month:

May $1000

June $1,000

July..................................$3,000

August.............................$3,000

September $3,000

October $3,500

November $3,500

December $4,000

January $4,500

February $5,000

March...............................$6,000

April.................................$7,600

Ultimate Vision: I want to have at least five different products that I am successfully marketing.

Mentors: I'll meet with my business mentor monthly and my internet marketing coach weekly on the phone.

Giving Back: I will give 10% of my net income to my church and help them generate revenue by putting their bookstore online.

I'll use Christine's plan as an opportunity to introduce a great planning system. It's a combination of the ABC, 123 System I've been using for 15 years and the RPM system I learned from Tony Robbins.

We'll focus our attention on the first month of Christine's plan, from the current date to her business launch date.

First I'll list the steps in the order that she developed them (in other words, as she thought them up). Then we'll prioritize and organize the steps into a comprehensive plan:

Steps to Accomplish

1. Find my first Product to market
2. Secure licensing agreement
3. Find second product and get agreement
4. Research other products
5. Develop sales letter for web site
6. Publish web site
7. Print business cards
8. Write 5 intro emails to drive traffic to site
9. Build first 1000 names on list
10. Build list to 5000 and beyond
11. Start marketing campaign
12. Secure URLs
13. Meet with Marketing Mentor weekly
14. Decide on domain names
15. Get merchant account
16. Meet with Business Coach monthly
17. Set up corporation
18. Set up operating account
19. Buy office supplies
20. Overture - pay per click
21. Google Ad words pay per click
22. J.V. 5 lists with 5,000 names or more
23. Get list JV agreements signed
24. Decide on my own product to develop
25. Buy Quick Books
26. Set up book keeping
27. Develop the product itself
28. Set up first teleclass
29. Get teleconference company and 100 lines
30. Get "800" number
31. Pre-record order message
32. Get letterhead

Get Yourself Organized

Christina realized that she has a lot to do in a relatively short amount of time. The only way she could accomplish all that's needed is to get organized. So she spent about an hour doing just that.

The first step in the ABC, 123 System is to put each task into a category. "A's" are the most important items, "B's" are next and "C's" are things like errands—they need to get done, but their impact is minimal. Notice that the categories have to do with the relative impact or importance of the items, NOT their urgency.

A good example of this is a ringing phone. It seems urgent in the moment, but depending on who is on the line, it could be a complete waste of your time. You need to be more discerning about how you invest your time.

Once each item is categorized, you can assign it a priority by number. It will look like this: A-1, A-2 A-3; B-1, B-2, C-1, etc. Years ago I had a partner who was really struggling in her effort to get things accomplished. I suggested that she use this system and she blurted out "I am—that's part of the problem. Everything is so important, I don't know where to start!" I asked to see her planner and immediately found the problem: EVERYTHING on the page was marked "A-1". No wonder she was frustrated!

The next step is to apply the "RPM" component which stands for "results", "purpose" and "momentum". What I'll do is write down the result I want to produce, and the purpose of the major steps to help keep me reminded, and then build momentum moving forward. The column marked "lev" is for things you want to leverage or delegate to someone else.   Here's Christina's new action list (I've left the original item numbers for reference purposes):

Lev	Day	PRI	Action	Result	Purpose
			Master Plan - 20XX May		
	M	A-1	6. Meet with Biz Coach re: Plan		To get my business off to a powerful start
	M	A-2	13. Meet with Marketing Mentor	I'm ready to start developing my new address	Ditto
	M	A-3	1. Find the first product to market	To secure a product I'm confident in and proud to be associated with.	To develop my first income stream
	T	A-4	2. Secure licensing agreement		
	T	A-5	5. Develop sales letter for web site		
	T	A-6	14. Decide on domain names		
	T	A-7	9. Build first 1000 names on list		To be ready to launch my marketing campaign
	W	A-8	12. Secure URLs		
	W	A-9	15. Apply for Merchant Account		So I can take orders

Lev	Day	PRI	Action	Result	Purpose
	W-TH	A-10	8. Write 5 intro emails to drive traffic to site		
	Th	A-11	22. Find J.V.'s - 5 list of 5000+		To jump-start my list
	Th	A-12	23. Get JV Agreements signed		
	Th	A-13	13. Meet again with Marketing Mentor		To fine tune my marketing efforts
	Th	A-14	20. Set up Overture Pay Per Click		Build the list
	F	A-15	21. Set up Google Ad words		Ditto
	F-S	A-16	30. Get "800" number		
	F-S	A-17	29. Get teleconference company and 100 lines		
	S	A-18	28. Set up first teleclass date		
	S	A-19	10. Start building my list to 5000		
		A-20	6. Publish web site		

Lev	Day	PRI	Action	Result	Purpose
		A-21	11. Start marketing campaign		
		A-22	31. Pre-record order message		
		A-23	4. Research other products		To start developing additional streams of income
		A-24	3. Find other products to market		Ditto
		A-25	24. Decide on my product to develop		
		A-26	27. Develop my own product		To maximize my business freedom
		B-1	17. Set up corporation		To protect myself and ensure max tax benefit
		B-2	18. Set up operating account		
		B-3	25. Buy Quickbooks		
Bk		B-4	26. Set up book keeping		To keep finances organized
P		B-5	7. Print business cards		
P		B-6	35. Get letterhead		
		C	19. Buy office supplies		

Can you see how much more organized things are at this point? Christina immediately feels more confident that she can success-fully complete her plan. Each task is categorized and numbered and all she has to do is follow her road map each day. Of course, she's able to modify her plan as she goes along, based on her actual results and progress.

Christina is working by herself, so there aren't many things that she can delegate—other than the bookkeeping and printing. When she hires an assistant s/he will be able to take care of many of the kinds of things in the "A" list, as well as most of the "B" list and the entire "C" list. And, she has inserted purpose statements next to the most important items to help keep her motivated and on task.

In summary, it's incredibly important to put together a realistic and workable plan. Don't do it for show by using some "canned" business plan software or knocking off one from the internet. Make your plan real. Make it viable. Get input from your mentors. Use it to avoid the major problems and solve other problems BEFORE they occur. It doesn't have to be fancy, it has to be powerful.

Then, break it down into bite size pieces. Remember "inch by inch it's a cinch." In other words, implement a weekly to-do list and a daily to do-list. Update your task list each evening as you finish the day's work. This will give your subconscious mind a chance to work things out overnight.

Take Action

1. Put together your first plan outline. Focus on the "big picture". Use the Category headings in the two sample plans as a guide.

2. Next, make a list of all the necessary steps you can think of—BIG and small. Ask your mentors to help you fill in the blanks.

3. Next, complete your first weekly plan and break it down further into a daily task plan.

4. Continue to meet with your mentors regularly to stay on course.

Resources

System

RPM planner by Tony Robbins

Audio Coarse

Time Management by Brian Tracy

:01
One Minute Review
You've Gotta Have a Plan

1. Develop a simple, written plan for your business as early on as possible.

2. The plan should cover the major aspects of your business including marketing, operations, finances and goals.

3. Develop several backup plans for each major area in case things don't go as expected.

4. Regularly compare your actual progress with your planned milestones and make appropriate adjustments.

5. Delegate everything that does not require your personal attention so you can focus on the "big ticket" items.

Bonus chapter 12

Tilt the Tax Laws in Your Favor

The single most important key to my business success
is a working knowledge of the tax code.
-Bill Gates

Having your own business opens the door to enormous tax benefits. Tax benefits that most business people don't even know about. Tax benefits that can save you tens of thousands of dollars.

But, before I go any further, I want to make sure that I'm understood.

I didn't say that the reason to go into business was to get the tax benefits. In fact, I made this one of the last chapters of this book in order to avoid that perception.

One main reason to have a business is to generate lasting wealth. Another main reason to have a business is the freedom it gives you. Another main reason to have a business is the creativity it inspires.

The tax benefits are ancillary. But what a huge benefit they are!

Let's start with a clear understanding that everything I teach about tax savings is above board. Its right out of the tax code. No grey areas or red flags to worry about.

You see, decades ago, the U.S. Supreme Court (the highest court in the country) issued a ruling that said "it is the Constitutional right of every American to arrange their affairs so as to minimize the amount of taxes they pay".

Did you catch that? They didn't say it was a good idea. They didn't say it was prudent planning. They said that its your <u>Constitutional right</u>. In the tax law world, it doesn't get any better than that.

Properly understood and utilized, the tax code is the business person's best friend. Yet, for some reason, most people are taught to fear the "tax man." Bad things happen when you mess with the IRS. That's true, but the operative phrase here is "mess with".

Its like the police. Growing up, I had a fear of cops. I guess I heard stories or news reports about cops gone bad. Or, in talking to friends or acquaintances who might have had a brush with the law, they'd put a spin on the story and lay blame on the cops, instead of taking responsibility for their own actions.

They'd say, "I was minding my own business and he pulled me over and gave me a ticket". They'd omit the fact that they were speeding.

They'd say, "Oh they just have it out for young people in cars". They'd omit the fact that they were joy riding with the car stereo blasting and open beer containers.

The tax man works in a similar way. If you fail to report income, you'll get snagged. If you lie on your return, you'll pay penalties and interest. (Note, usually the penalties and interest end up being much more than the original underpayment. For example, I've seen underpayments of $10,000 grow to $30,000 or $40,000 after penalties and interest accrue).

But if you do things properly, the tax code is an incredible asset to you.

You see, this country's political and economic systems are based on two overriding principles: democracy and capitalism. Our system of government has always favored entrepreneurs and business people. America was founded by entrepreneurs and business people, so that shouldn't come as any surprise. The tax code contains built-in government subsidies that are designed to help you and your business succeed. If you follow the rules, you get the benefit of them, worry free.

Let me explain. Imagine that you're on the highway during rush hour. You're stuck in bumper to bumper traffic—crawling along in your car at 3 miles per hour. You're tired, frustrated and bored. You call friends and family on your cell phone to break up the monotony. You blast the radio. Anything to distract yourself.

Then, out of the corner of your eye, you see a car go cruising by at 55 miles an hour. "Where did he come from?" you ask yourself. Then another one goes by, and another. You're confused, wondering how come you're stuck on a traffic jam and their well on their way to being home with their family.

Then, you see a sign in the distance. As you approach, the sign gets more clear. It says "HOV" lane. And it tells you the associated rule "This is the <u>H</u>igh <u>O</u>ccupancy <u>V</u>ehicle lane. It is reserved for cars with 2 passengers or more."

The tax code is like the financial HOV lane. It has an entirely different set of rules for business owners than for non business owners. You need to learn those rules and put them to work for you. If you do, you'll be able to build lasting wealth much, much faster.

In my experience, even successful and savvy business owners are only getting about 10% percent of the tax benefits they are entitled to. That means they (and you) are shunning 90% of the possible tax benefits. The net result is that you are throwing away thousands and thousands of dollars each year, unnecessarily. Its time for you to recoup some of that money, wouldn't you say?

The Supreme Court issued a second ruling that was startling to me when I first read it. According to the Supreme Court, there are two tax systems in this Country; one for the educated and one for the uneducated. And the incredible thing is that you get to choose which one you want to be in.

Here's what the uneducated system looks like:

Income
- Taxes
What you can live on.

In other words, your taxes are deducted from your income and you must live on what's left over. This is the W-2 system. Let's look at the repercussions of being in this system.

Take out a recent pay stub. You'll notice that the top line is your gross pay. Let's say $1,000. But you can't live on the $1,000 because you have taxes to pay. In fact, the next three lines of your pay check are the taxes that are withheld. Federal Taxes of up to 39%. State taxes of up to 9.6%. City taxes (if you work or live within a City) of up to 3%. And then there is FICA, or social security tax of 15.65 % (you pay half and your employer matches it.)

All tolled, the average American pays between 42% and 55% in taxes. Let me simplify that, you are giving up approximately 50% of your income in the form of income taxes. This doesn't include sales tax, property tax, excise tax, gasoline tax or the myriad other taxes. These are just income-based taxes.

Let's put numbers to our illustrations:

$100,000	Income
- $ 50,000	Taxes (approx.)
$ 50,000	Spendable Income

Look back at the quote that opened this chapter. This is what Bill Gates was referring to. He knew that the secret to building wealth was not making a lot of money or working harder. He knew that the secret was keeping more of what he earned, because its not how much you make, its what you keep that counts.

It's a lot harder to get ahead when you're paying upwards of 50% of your hard-earned money to the "tax man". Yet, as I said earlier, there is a better way. Our tax system was designed to encourage and assist entrepreneurs and business owners, which leads us to the "other" tax system in this Country. The educated tax system which looks like this:

Income
- Expenses
Taxable Amount

This is the tax system of business owners, yet most business people don't fully appreciate it. Not even close.

For most business people, the illustration breaks down like this:

$100,000	**Income**
- $10,000	**Business Expenses**
$ 90,000	**Taxable Income**
$45,000	**Taxes (approx.)**

Now, $45,000 in taxes is better than $50,000. But as a business owner, you can do so much better.

One of the big mistakes I see business people making is relying on their accountant or CPA to "take care of their tax problem". Think about it, isn't that one of the things you rely on your accountant for? After all, that's who "does your taxes" isn't it? But this is bad business.

Here's the problem. Your accountant or C.P.A. doesn't consider it his/her job to find you every available deduction and never did. In fact, that's not their job. (if this comes as a shock to you, urge you to call him/her). But you better be sitting down. Think about it. Would you go to the dentist if you had a pain in your foot? Would you go to a chiropractor if you had a toothache? If you are expecting the wrong professionals to help solve a problem, it's not their fault that they can't help you.

So, if it's not the accountant's job to reduce your taxes, whose job is it? It's your job! You've been too busy being entrepreneurial, doing the next deal and growing your business to pay proper attention. And it's costing you a ton of money.

I said earlier that even the most successful and savvy business people who I interview are getting only about 10% of the benefits they are entitled to. That's not very different from beginning entrepreneurs.

In fact, for most business people, taxes are their single largest expense. But not for you and not for long.

My team and I have been able to uncover over 300 individual deductions that are available to business owners. Most of them are severely underutilized.

It's not that they are risky. It's not that they fall into the grey area. It's because you don't know them and as we've discussed, it's not the job of accountants and C.P.A.'s to find them for you, so they lay buried in the tax code. That was the secret that Bill Gates was referring to. By learning more about these little known tax secrets, he was able to reduce his taxes to single digits. That's less than 10%,

The first step in using more of the deductions available to you in the tax code is to convert more of your existing expenses into legitimate business expenses. In other words, there are many things that you use personal funds on—on a daily, weekly or monthly basis, that can be written off by your business.

Let's revisit our illustration.

$ 100,000	Income
- $10,000	(Typical) Business Expenses
$ 90,000	Taxable Income
- 30,000	("Secret" Deductions)
$60,000	(Your New Taxable Income)
$30,000	(Approx. Taxes)

That's a savings of $20,000. $20,000 you can spend on anything you want. $20,000 you can use to finance your business growth. $20,000 you can do whatever you want with. That's working smarter, not harder. And that's just the beginning.

When we started working together, Carol had been in business for five years. Her two corporations yielded her a net (taxable) income of $50,000. Her taxes we about $12,000. This broke down into $7,500 in FICA and $4,500 in state and federal taxes.

Like many of our new clients, Carol felt she was already taking all the available deductions. In fact, her C.P.A. told her he was certain of it. So, she wanted to focus on other things, like asset protection and marketing. Now, these are really important in your overall plan, but I didn't want her to lose out on some big tax savings.

We set up a conference call so we could review her tax situation together. After some preliminaries, we got down to business. During our 15 minute phone call, I suggested 3 strategies. As we reviewed each one, I asked her C.P.A. to calculate the savings. Before we hung up, I added up the figures and by his calculations, just these 3 strategies alone would save her $11,200.

The point isn't that I somehow "one-upped" the C.P.A. Remember, I said earlier that this isn't your C.P.A.'s responsibility, its yours as a business owner. My point in bringing up this example is to point out to you that despite your best efforts, you are almost certainly overpaying your taxes. The savings can be enormous.

Let me show you some of them and the impact they can have on your business. These figures are considered conservative; your savings may be significantly greater.

Strategy 1: Home office deductions.
Deductions including phones, equipment, furnishings, etc. ....$1,000 per year

Supplies ....$2,000 per year

Strategy 2: Entertainment.
Meals—assuming $20/wk for 50 weeks - $1000 x 50% ....$ 500 per year

Sales presentations $100 each - 1 per month $1,200 @ 100% ....$1,200 per year

Business parties $400 ea. X 2 parties @ 100% .... $ 800 per year

Business entertaining $100 ea. x 6 .... $ 600 per year

Get-togethers x 100%

Strategy 3: Vacations and travel.
$2,000 per vacation x one vacation........................$2,000 per year

Strategy 4: Automobile Expenses.

5,000 business miles x 33 cents................................$1,650 per year

Strategy 5: Your children's college and wedding (or first house).

$7,000 per child x 2 children (average)................$14,000 per year

Strategy 6: Education and Seminar Expenses.

Assuming 2 seminars per year @ $500 each.........$ 1,000 per year

Strategy 7: Medical Reimbursement Plan.

Average savings for a family of 3.........................$ 2,750 per year

Strategy 8: Business Gifts.

Average $1,500...$ 1,500 per year

Other:

Average deductions per year: (w/ Children).....................$29,000

(w/oChildren) $15,000

Tax savings: (w/children).......................................$10,000 approx.

(w/o children) ....$ 5,000 approx.

In addition, if you are properly structured, you can write off all of your medical insurance and health care (including dental, chiropractic, wellness care, eye care, etc. for you and your spouse, the cost of travel and season tickets, moving expenses, gym equipment and life insurance. And this just scratches the surface.

A common mistake is focusing on the item that you want to deduct. For example, you may want to deduct your auto expenses, your desk and equipment or your cell phone. While the deductibility of some items is obvious (and commonplace) others are not so apparent.

When I speak at live events, I like to give the example of something innocuous, like pizza. I'll ask the audience, if you called up your accountant right now and asked her if you could deduct a pizza, she'd probably ask you if you had gone mad. "Pizza, you can't deduct a pizza, for crying out loud", she'd say.

Ok. Now let's look at pizza, from a different perspective. Suppose you take a business associate to an Italian restaurant to discuss business and have pizza and a couple of beers. Now, suddenly the same pizza (and the beers) are fifty percent deductible.

Which brings us to an important point. It's not the item, it's the circumstances and applying the proper rules. So, from now on don't ask "is this deductible"? Instead, ask "How is this deductible?" The answer may be very different.

Ready for some more? Here is a list of what my friend Al Allen calls the Golden Tax Secrets for corporations.

IRC #		Golden Tax Secrets	Amount	Your $'s
<u>79</u>	1.	**Group Term Life Insurance.** You can receive up to $50,000 in coverage and the premium is not included in your gross income, and it is 100% deductible to your corporation.	$50,000.00	
<u>74</u>	2.	**Achievement and Awards for Safety and Longevity.** These awards have to be in writing and can be up to $1,600 each. In a family corporation, both the husband and wife could receive the awards annually. The wife might receive the Longevity Award because she has been with the company since its inception. The husband might receive the Safety Award because he maintains a safe work environment. These awards are tax-free deductions for the company.	$1,600.00	
<u>105</u>	3.	**Health Insurance**. If you already have a health insurance program, the corporation can reimburse you for any expenses paid.	NO LIMIT	
<u>106</u>	4.	**Insured Medical Plans.** Your corporation can pay 100% of your medical plan. The amount is not included in your gross pay	100%	
<u>119</u>	5.	**Meals and Lodging.** When your meals and lodging are furnished by the employer (your corporation) and you are required to live in the house and eat on the premises, then they are paid for by the corporation as a business expense and are tax deductible. These are no limits to the amount spent for meals and lodging. Strict compliance with the code is necessary.	100%	
<u>125</u>	6.	**Cafeteria Plan.** Your corporation can provide a cafeteria plan, which may include a combination of the above sections. This does not affect your gross income.	100%	
<u>129</u>	7.	**Dependent Care.** Your corporation can provide you up to $5,000 a year for dependent care and it's not part of your gross income.	$5,000	
<u>127</u>	8.	**Educational Assistance.** Your allotment is up to $5,250, and is not part of your gross income.	$5,250	
<u>162</u>	9.	**Seminars.** Expenses (including meals and lodging) for business related seminars are 100% tax deductible to the corporation and are not included as part of your income.	100%	
<u>132(e)</u>	10.	**"De-minimis fringes."** This includes any property or service the value of which is so small that accounting is unreasonable such as coffee, company barbeques at the office and other miscellaneous expenses. Frequency must be considered according to the code.	Open	
<u>217</u>	11.	**Moving Expenses.** All reasonable moving expenses except meals can be paid for and are not included in your gross pay.	100%	
132(h)(s)	12.	**Physical Fitness.** You can have a physical fitness facility on your premises totally paid for by the corporation.	100%	
<u>179</u>	13.	**Depreciation.** You can deduct or depreciate $18,000 of your office equipment in a single year. Automobiles are not included in this. They need to be placed on a five-year depreciation plan.	$18,000	
<u>243</u>	14.	**Dividends.** If your corporation is receiving dividends from another corporation such as stocks, mutual funds, etc. You can eliminate 70 to 100% of the gain. You are only taxed on 20%. If your company received $1000 in capital gains, $800 is forgiven.	80/20	
<u>2501</u>	15.	<u>**Stock Freezing**</u>		
<u>331</u>	16.	<u>**Inter-Corporate Transfers of Assets**</u>		
<u>221</u>	17.	<u>**Production of Income**</u>		

Case Study #1: Family of 5, Husband is a handy man. Wife is a part-time student and part-time bookkeeper in family business. Her Child #1 is age 15. His Child #2 is age 10. Their Child #3 is age 5. They own their home with $8,000 per year mortgage interest and $2,000 per year in property taxes. Medical insurance is $200 per mo. Child #2 has braces at a cost of 1000 per year.

CASE #1	Individual		Corporation	
Gross Income		$50,000.00		$50,000.00
Business Deductions	Sched. C	23,500.00		58,000.00
	Cost of Goods	15,000.00	Cost of Goods	15,000.00
	Truck Dep./Gas	8,500.00	Husband's salary	12,000.00
			Wife's Salary	6,000.00
			Payroll Taxes	1,800.00
			Wife's Education	5,250.00
			Child #1 *	590.00
			Child #2 *	590.00
			Child #3 *	590.00
			Group Life (h/w) Co.	500.00
			Med. Ins.	2,400.00
			Med. Reimbursement	1,000.00
			Truck @ .29 mi.	5,800.00
			Home Office Rent $3 per sq. ft.	6,480.00
Adjusted Income		26,500.00		8,000.00
Family Deductions		25,722.00		16,500.00
Taxable Income		778.00		Personal 1,500.00
Taxes	Total Personal	3,861.00	Total Personal Payroll	2,025.00
	Self Employ	0.00		225.00
		3861.00		1,800.00
Tax Savings			$1,836.00	
Taxes per day		$10.67		$ 4.93
Tax Carryover		$0.00		$8,000.00

Note Investment Profits from Tax Savings: Invest $900 per year in an IRA. Get additional $135 tax savings. In 20 years at 9% interest IRA will yield $50,000. Add to that the $1071 per year in tax savings, and you will total approximately $73,000 saved by incorporating. *Independent Contractors.

Case Study #2: In this example, the income is now $75,000. I'm not going to go through all the deductions again. I will point out that the salaries have increased. The children's salaries have also increased and the savings are put into IRA's for the children. The difference in tax savings between an individual and a corporation is awesome. The family will save over $6,000 in taxes this year. Investing some of this into their IRA's they also get an additional $1,120 in tax savings but they will end up with over $278,000 saved by incorporating if invested over a 20 year period.

Note that Case Study #2 is the same family as Case 1 except the income is higher and the employees get achievement awards.

CASE #2	Individual		Corporation	
Gross Income		$75,000.00		$75,000.00
Business Deductions	Sched. C	30,500.00		73,020.00
	Cost of Goods	22,000.00	Cost of Goods	22,000.00
	Truck Dep./Gas	8,500.00	Husband's salary	12,000.00
			Wife's Education	5,250.00
			Payroll Taxes	1,800.00
			Child #1 Salary	3,800.00
			Child #2 Salary	3,800.00
			Child #3 *	590.00
			Group Life (h/w) Co.	500.00
			Med. Ins.	2,400.00
			Med. Reimbursement	1,000.00
			Truck @ .29 mi.	5,800.00
			Home Office Rent $3 per sq. ft.	6,480.00
			$400 achievement awards (H/w/C1/C2)	1,600.00
Adjusted Income		44,500.00		1,980.00
Family Deductions		25,994.00		16,500.00
Taxable Income		18,506.00	Corporate	1,980.00
			Personal	1,500.00
Taxes	Total	9,064.00	Total	2,322.00
	Personal	2,776.00	Corp.	297.00
	Self Employ	6,288.00	Personal	225.00
			Payroll	1,800.00
Tax Savings		$6,156.00		
Taxes per Day		$24.83		$7.96
Tax Saved per Mo.				$513.00

Note Investment Profits from Tax Savings: Invest $2,000 per year for each parent in IRA's. Get additional $1,120 tax savings. In 20 years at 9% interest IRA's will yield $223,000. Add to that the $1,071 per year in tax savings, and you will save approximately $278,000 saved by incorporating.

* Independent Contractor

Case Studies #3 & #4: You will note even greater savings occur in Case Studies #3 and #4. I would like to point out in Case Study #4 the couple's salaries have increased to $135,000 in gross income. If you look at the things that have changed, the wife now has a car. Both have higher incomes, and everybody receives awards. A SEP IRA in the amount of $6,000 is deductible to the corporation and not part of the income of the individuals. The family's tax savings are $18,270. This is beyond the SEP IRA and all those other benefits that are being taken care of within the corporation. Read the bottom line which is in the footnotes; these people will have savings of $2,451,000, at 9%. That's $2,451,000 from invested income just from tax savings from running their business as a corporation and utilizing the tax codes available to them.

CASE #3	Individual		Corporation	
Gross Income		$80,000.00		$80,000.00
Business Deductions	Sched. C	22,000.00		78,270.00
	Cost of Goods	13,500.00	Cost of Goods	13,500.00
	Truck Dep./Gas	8,500.00	Husband's Salary	12,000.00
			Wife's Salary	12,000.00
			Payroll Taxes	2,400.00
			Child #1 Salary	5,800.00
			Child #2 Salary	5,800.00
			Child #3 *	590.00
			Group Life (h/w) Co.	500.00
			Med. Ins.	2,400.00
			Med. Reimbursement	1,000.00
			Truck @ .29 mi.	5,800.00
			Home Office Rent $3 per sq. ft.	6,480.00
			Awards $1,600.00	3,200.00
			C1 & C2 Camp	2,000.00
			C3 Child Care	3,000.00
			Car for Wife	1,800.00
Adjusted Income		58,000.00		1,730.00
Family Deductions		26,950.00		16,500.00
Taxable Income		31,050.00		1,730.00
Taxes	Total	12,173.00	Total	3,784.00
	Personal	3,978.00	Corp.	259.00
	Self Employ	8,195.00	Personal	1,125.00
			Payroll	2,400.00
Tax Savings		$8,389.00		
Taxes per Day		$33.25		$ 10.36
Tax Saved per Mo.				$699.08

Note Investment Profits from Tax Savings: Invest $2,000 per year per parent in IRA's. Get additional $1,120 tax savings. In 20 years at 90% interest IRA's will yield $223,000. Invest $2,000 per year for 3 years in IRA for Child #1, $2,000 per year for 8 year for Child #2. The Value of children's IRA's at age 65 will be $317,000 for Child #1 and $1,380,000 for Child #2. The total for the family will amount to $2,019,180.

* Independent Contractor

CASE #4	Individual		Corporation	
Gross Income		$135,000.00		$135,000.00
Business Deductions	Sched. C	35,000.00		114,870.00
	Cost of Goods	26,500.00	Cost of Goods	26,500.00
	Truck Dep./Gas	8,500.00	Husband's Salary	20,000.00
			Wife's Salary	20,000.00
			Payroll Taxes	4,000.00
			Child #1 Salary	5,800.00
			Child #2 Salary	5,800.00
			Child #3 *	590.00
			Group Life (h/w) Co.	500.00
			Med. Ins.	2,400.00
			Med. Reimbursement	1,000.00
			Truck @ .29 mi.	5,800.00
			Home Office Rent $3 per sq. ft.	6,480.00
			Awards $1,600.00	3,200.00
			C1 & C2 Camp	2,000.00
			C3 Child Care	3,000.00
			Car for Wife	1,800.00
			SEP	6,000.00
Adjusted Income		100,000.00		20,130.00
Family Deductions		29,915.00		16,500.00
Taxable Income		70,085.00	Corp.	20,130.00
			Personal	23,500.00
Taxes	Total	28,814.00	Total	10,544.00
	Personal	14,684.00	Corp.	3,019.00
	Self Employ	14,130.00	Personal	3,525.00
			Payroll	4,000.00
Tax Savings		$18,270.00		
Taxes per Day		$78.94		$ 28.89
Tax Saved per Mo.				$1,522.00

Note Investment Profits from Tax Savings: Invest $2,000 per year per parent in IRA's. Get additional $1,120 tax savings. In 20 years at 90% interest IRA's will yield $223,000. Invest $2,000 per year for 3 years in IRA for Child #1, $2,000 per year for 8 year for Child #2. The Value of children's IRA's at age 65 will be $317,000 for Child #1 and $1,380,000 for Child #2. The parents will also have a SEP plan and fund it at 15% of salary of a total of $6,000 per year in 20 years to total $334,600. These total $2,303,880.00

Add the extra from taxes of $11,225 per year. The total for the family will amount to $2,251,940 from their tax savings alone.

* Independent Contractor

Again, the purpose of your business is to earn a profit and to enjoy the freedom, wealth, status and all the other benefits associated with being a business owner. But the tax benefits are substantial. Part of your overall success plan should be to put them to good use.

Take Action

1. Review your taxes for the last 3 years and calculate what percentage of your income was paid to Uncle Sam.

2. If you are paying more than 10% in taxes contact Pathfinder Business Strategies LLC and get a free tax strategy session with one of our senior tax specialists.>

3. Call 1-800-505-3329 and avail yourself of one of Pathfinder's tax saving, wealth enhancing coaching programs: Silver, Gold, Platinum and Diamond Mentoring Programs

Resources

Website

www.pfbs.com

:01
One Minute Review
Tilt the Tax Laws in Your Favor

1. The tax laws have been set up to favor business owners. Its your right to get the most our of them.

2. If you follow the rules, you can get the benefits without worrying about upsetting the "tax man"

3. You must properly document your deductions so that you "audit proof" you records.

4. Many of your existing personal can be business deductions.

5. Don't ask "Is this deductible?" Ask a more powerful question" How can this be deductible?"

chapter 13

Parting Thoughts

> Learning is the beginning of wealth.
> Learning is the beginning of health.
> Learning is the beginning of spirituality.
> Searching and learning is where
> the miracle process all begins.
> -Jim Rohn

My purpose for writing this book was to give you a blue print for business success. Having examined the blueprint, it's almost time for you to begin building the financial future of your dreams. I truly believe that if you apply its principles you can go from Zero (or where ever you currently find yourself) to Success (as you define the word) within twelve to twenty four months.

That being said, there are some loose ends that I want to tie off before leaving you to your work. Some of them could be chapters in their own right; perhaps I'll cover them in more detail in another book. Yet when you weave them into the ten primary steps, they form a strong fabric that can be used to create a successful business, one that reflects who you are, what your life is about and what's important to you.

Attitude

Attitude has so many components and collectively those components color everything we do. From what we perceive to how we interpret it, process it and respond to it both long term and short term it's all about attitude.

Perception

I've come to believe that in many ways there is no such thing as reality; there is only YOUR reality. Now, that may not be the case for most tangible things (you either drive a blue car or a red car—there's little room for interpretation) but it certainly is the case for things like our emotions, philosophy and perspective.

You will approach things differently if you perceive the glass as half empty than if you perceive it as half full. And how you approach a situation alters everything else about it—even the ultimate outcome for you.

I was recently coaching a young man (Greg) who was about to start (actually re-start) college. His parents had been divorced for some time, and now at age 20, he was already living on his own. He was struggling financially and emotionally, had become rebellious, and the path he had chosen for himself during prior years was getting him nowhere fast. Six months before, his father had offered to help him out financially as long as he enrolled in college and attained reasonable grades.

About half way through the semester, he became overwhelmed and fearful that his father would withdraw his support. Greg opted not to tell anyone that he had stopped going to his classes.

Inevitably, his mother and father discovered the truth. Yet, they remained supportive; in fact, after recommending some changes in Greg's habits, his father offered to pay his rent, give him money for food, pay his tuition and the cost of books, give him a car with insurance and relieve him totally of the financial burden of supporting himself while he studied. His mother helped him register, apply for financial aid and find student housing. His parents had only a few requirements—they told him he had to apply himself, do what he said he would do, and be honest with them—in good times and bad.

The night before he was to leave for college, he had errands to run and a few friends to say goodbye to. He headed out in the car promising to be back by 11 p.m.

At 1 a.m. the phone rang. Greg's father had called his mother to see if she knew where Greg was. "That #!^&%#@ kid was supposed to be back here at 11 o'clock. Where the heck do you suppose he is? "

Before she could respond, Greg's father went into a tirade. "He's probably out partying with those #@%*! friends of his—I ask him to do one thing, just get home at a reasonable hour so he can be ready for the long drive tomorrow and he can't even do that. Who knows where he is… that's it, I'm taking the car back and I'm not giving him a nickel for school. If he wants to be so independent, he can find a way to put himself through school!"

And in five minutes, the whole family was in a state of crisis and Greg's future was right back in the gutter.

When I spoke with Greg the next day, he had all kinds of stories to tell me. He was sick and tired of his father's hot temper, he was only a couple of hours late, what's the big deal, he wasn't going to let anyone control him and college wasn't for him anyway.

I let him vent for a while, then took the opportunity to point out a few things. Without his dad he had no car. That was because his car was confiscated after he lost his drivers license six month's before because of excessive speeding tickets. He opted to drop out of school because he was failing his classes—probably the result of too much partying with friends.

He was just fired from a clerical job with an accounting firm because he insisted on parking in one of the parking spots reserved for clients. Just two months prior, he spent the night in the hospital after being mugged by a group of thugs. "That wasn't my fault", he insisted. And only a week ago, his car insurance was canceled because he failed to pay his premiums on time.

There was more, but I knew from his expression that I had made my point. And now, he was on the verge once again of blowing it all—all because of a poor attitude.

I pointed out that because of his actions, a lot of people were being harmed. That his latest misstep was damaging his future chances and that he and he alone had the power to alter that. And it all boiled down to his attitude.

His perception was that those in authority (his dad, the police, the insurance company, his teachers) wanted to control him. He interpreted that authority as an intrusion into his freedom. He processed the situation out of anger and responded by cutting himself off from others and "doing things my own way". The problem was that "his way" didn't work.

Thankfully, after a little crisis intervention, he was able to turn things around. I offered him a different way to perceive the situation—namely that his father and the other people in authority actually had his best interest in mind. Yet, with his recent track record, he gave few people any reason to trust him or take him at his word. This allowed him to interpret their actions and suggestions as guidance instead of brute force. He began to process the situation differently. As a result, he responded by realizing that it was HIS responsibility to come clean, to apologize where appropriate and to clean up his mistakes.

Within 48 hours, he had enrolled in college, selected his classes, found a place to live, insured his car and committed to a game plan that was more likely to result in his success.

The key steps are to ask powerful questions (i.e. *How can I?* Instead of *why can't I?*). Look for the lessons in the adversity, be coachable (keep an open mind) and develop a better plan and stick to it.

Commit to Life-long Education

When I passed the bar exam, I figured I was done with education—at least for a while. I had completed four years of college in three years, graduated with honors and completed three years of law school while serving as a legal intern. I was ready to get to work.

Why do you think they call it practice?

Soon I was faced with business decisions, legal decisions to make for my clients, marketing decisions, administrative decisions and life decisions—all in areas that I had little or no training. I soon realized that college and law school merely provided me with the minimum training required to enter the field. I had a whole lifetime of learning ahead of me.

And that's what I committed to. I took a special program at the bar association for new attorneys, then I started taking continuing education classes in my areas of interest—before they were mandatory. I've read hundreds and hundreds of books, listened to thousands of hours of tapes, completed over $250,000 of on-going education and seminars.

I always have training tapes and CDs in the car; there is NEVER a time when I don't. I consider my car to be a "university on wheels" and I am always enrolled.

As Mark Victor Hansen says, "You need to become positively addicted to education and personal development." Yes, it's an addiction, but you might as well be addicted to some good stuff, in light of all the negative things the world has to offer.

And, in case you're wondering, I continue to educate myself and so do my students. In fact, I just got off the phone with one of my mentors, and he's on his way to a seminar this weekend.

I think it was Brian Tracy who put it this way: If you read 12 books, you can speak with confidence about a particular subject. If you read 12 books on that subject per year (that's one per month), you can become an authority in about five years.

If you read 20 books a year, you'll be a leading authority in three years. And if you read 50 books a year (that's one per week), you'll be a true expert in one to three years.

Keep reading, growing, listening and learning.

Capitalizing Your Business

Truly this is the subject of a whole book. It's a hugely important topic to business owners. That's because *one of the leading causes of business failures is undercapitalization*—in other words, not having enough cash to get by.

This book is not geared toward people who intend to take a company public. It's for the small business owner.

So, my first piece of advice is to consider a service or information based business instead of a traditional retail or manufacturing business—at least at first. That's because the capital requirements for service or information businesses is far lower than retail or manufacturing. Take a look at the table below:

Description of Needs	Service or Information	Manufacturing or Retail
Store or Plant	No	Yes
Inventory	No	Yes
Special Equipment	No	Yes
Employees	No	Yes

Each of these components requires capital—both up front (security deposits, stock, etc) and on an on-going basis. So, why not focus on a business that requires as little capital as possible? Incidentally, Internet based retail sales fills the bill as well.

Joint Ventures are another way of financing your business. Partner up with your suppliers and vendors and minimize your up front costs. For example, if you need to develop a database to sell your online information products do a J.V. with others who already have a list of prospects. Then, build that into an affiliate program for further leverage.

Same thing with special equipment—partner up or outsource the need. For example, recently I began a new marketing campaign that required staff to help prepare a series of mailers and an "auto-dialer" to confirm attendees a few days before a seminar we promoted. Rather than lay out $5,000 for the autodialing equipment and hiring and training the staff, I outsourced both requirements. For a total cost of a few hundred extra dollars, I got the entire project completed without having to lay out a lot of money.

Perhaps the biggest breakthrough I had regarding business capital was when I committed to financing the cost of operations completely from new business. That idea created a "paradigm shift" for me that changed the way I view my business.

In other words, in the old days, I would commit to spending a sum of money (say $10,000, $50,000, $100,000) to get a business up and running. I'd put together a budget for inventory, supplies, marketing, rent, salaries, etc and based on my projections, I'd calculate a break even date for the business. Sometimes the projection was months, sometimes it was years.

The problem is that if things don't go as planned, I'm $100,000 in the hole and the business is caput (I now refer to this as "tuition"). Instead, I now look to pay for much of the start up costs from pre-sales. This book is an example. It can cost tens of thousands of dollars to successfully write, edit, produce and market a book. We decided that before it was released to the public, we would partner with as many of the vendors as possible and pre-sell the book to a select group of people (starting with my students). That allowed us to offset much of the initial cost and launch the book successfully.

If you are selling a service or information product, you can do the same thing. Suppose you start a cleaning service (as one of my early students, Janine, did). We identified her target market—in this case local businesses. Then Janine committed to financing her entire business through proper marketing. First, she kept her day job. We knew it would pay the bills for the time being. Her initial goal was to get to $3,000 income per month so she could quit her job.

Next, she approached local business owners and offered them one free office cleaning. At the end of the free cleaning, once we determined that they were happy with the quality of service, we asked them to sign up for a twelve month program. Instead of paying $80 per week, she offered them a special discount of $25 each, twice a week if they prepaid 3 months worth and agreed to quarterly billing. She found that she could do 2 or 3 offices at night, after work and 7 on Saturday. In just a few weeks, Janine had filled up all her available slots and had $9,000 in pre-payments. She was making $2,000 per month from her business—two thirds of the way to achieving her goal of $3,000 per month.

Next, she cut back to half the number of hours at her job, and used the additional time to market her business—this time at closer to full price (we still had several incentive programs including a pre-payment option).

Her next step was to hire and train 2 part time employees. This cut into her revenue but gave her more time (and energy) to market her business. She also inspected the work of her employees to insure high quality standards.

Within nine months, Janine was able to leave her job. She had a full slate of customers and kept 2 part time cleaners gainfully employed. All this on a start up budget of next to nothing!

Multiple Streams of Income

Almost a decade ago, Robert Allen, author of *Nothing Down*, the first definitive guide to buying real estate with little or no money of your own, wrote a book called *Multiple Streams of Income*. Several years later, he wrote the follow-up called *Multiple Streams of Internet Income*. The book started a buzz in wealth building circles and at seminars around the world.

It rightfully outlined the importance of developing more than one stream of income—both offensively and defensively. **Offensively**, because multiple streams gave you a means of increasing your income through multiple streams; **Defensively**, because if one income stream dries up, you still have another (or several) to fall back on and rebuild.

Often, when I'm teaching at a seminar, a student will call out "Teach us about Multiple Streams of Income." I usually pause and smile and tell them to write down this sage piece of advice: "You can't have multiple streams of income unless you have one stream to start with." No kidding?

That may seem self evident, but there are many new wealth builders attempting to go into four or five businesses at once (You know who you are). You watch an infomercial about real estate investing and sign up for the course. One week later, your friend takes you to an MLM meeting and you get hooked. Then, you read about day traders pulling thousands and thousands of dollars out of the market and you decide to do that too. Any one of these businesses can take years to properly learn and do and somehow, you think you're going to do it all at once. Not likely!

Here is the key: develop one core stream of income first, before you even think of adding another. Build your core business. De-Bug it. Systematize it. Make it run without you. Then, if all is well, you can start to develop a second stream of income. If you are just starting out, it will probably take five years before you are ready to add a stream.

Then when you do add another stream, I suggest that you make it a natural offshoot of your existing business.

If you're a real estate investor, don't go out and start a restaurant. Add a variation to your investment strategies. If you do flips; add some rentals. If you build houses on spec, add foreclosures.

If you are a hair dresser, sell hair products—maybe you can develop your own. Later, you can write a book about hair care and create your own audio program.

Or maybe you are a musician and you do gigs for a living. Cut your own CD. Add an audio/video training course. Compile a song book. You get the idea.

Now the most important step: you must turn each of those streams of income into an independent source of revenue. Here's what I mean.

Back to the Hairdresser: Your core business is cutting hair. So, you develop your own line of hair products and sell them to your customers. That's a great start, but you must also market those products to non-customers. Try the web, mail order, ads in magazines, trade shows, flea markets...whatever. It's just a matter of marketing. Just don't rely solely on your own customers for that stream of income. Why?

Because what happens if you have to stop cutting hair? Maybe it's because of an illness, or you lose your lease, or you move or whatever. If only your hair product customers are your hair styling customers you are in trouble. Same thing with your video program—if your only video customers are your hair styling customers and you stop styling hair, you're back in the soup. All of your income streams dry up at once.

So, make each stream of income independent of the others. It will take time, but it will be well worth it.

One Last Point—I call it my 80% rule

I have noticed new wealth builders fall into a pattern. "John" hears about some new business opportunity—say buying foreclosures and he becomes fascinated. It seems interesting, even fun and something he is confident he can master. And, most importantly, it appears to be lucrative.

So, he buys the audio program and studies it. He is gaining confidence that with a little more training, he can actually do a deal. Then he decides to take the three day workshop. The workshop is great and John is inspired and ready to go. He's worked hard and invested a lot of time and money. It's time to do a deal. He's worked to the point where he's about eighty percent competent.

John goes to his first auction and gets the winning bid. He fixes up the property, just like he learned—new carpet, paint and some shrubs. Heck he did all the work himself. No point in sharing the wealth with some contractor.

He advertises the property and gets an offer but it's only for a couple of thousand more than he paid with the improvements. After paying for the ad and the lawyers fees, he barely made a profit. What went wrong, he asks? His family only makes things worse by saying things like, "I told you so."

Now comes the moment of truth. You see, in high school and college, a score of 80% is respectable. But in business 80% means you break even, or perhaps lose a little money. This is the real world.

John's next step will determine the ultimate outcome. Here's where we divide him into Smart John "SJ" and the Other John "OJ".

OJ gets dejected and decides that "this foreclosure stuff isn't for me". He turns on the T.V. that night and sees an infomercial for another business opportunity. This one is for a web business. He reasons that this is more his speed, so he buys the program. He studies it hard, and decides to take the workshop. He learns how to design a website and puts up his own home page. He's about eighty percent competent. But nothing happens. No sales. No Revenue. No Profits. So, OJ decides "this isn't for me".

That weekend he attends a trade show and learns about a new MLM. Greatest thing since sliced bread the speakers say. OJ agrees and so it goes.

Somewhere along the line OJ gives up and decides he's a failure and "those people were just taking advantage of me." Neither one is true.

Now, let's go through the process with Smart John "SJ".

SJ buys that foreclosure course and studies it. He goes to the workshop to learn more and get a mentor. When he's 80% competent, he does his first deal. He completes the process and makes almost nothing the first time around.

This time, SJ picks up the phone and calls his mentor. They go through the deal step by step and SJ learns where he fell a little short. He gets up to 85% before his second deal and this time he makes $5,000. Nothing to write home about but at least he's making money.

He calls up his mentor and learns a few more things he can improve on. This makes him about 90% competent and on his third deal he makes $10,000.

He keeps learning and by 95% he's making $15,000 - $20,000 per deal consistently. At 98% he's got a consistent, reliable stream of income and he becomes a master.

The same person using the same initial facts—but with two totally different outcomes.

It's your choice.

Take Action

1. Look for places where your attitude is holding you back. Resolve to improve yourself by working on one shortcoming at a time.

2. Commit to financing your business (especially if it's your first business) from pre-sales and new orders. Don't go into hock to start your first business. It's not necessary.

3. Develop your core business. Once that business is dependable and consistent, add additional streams of income one at a time, until each is dependable and consistent.

4. Learn from your mistakes. Learn from your mentors. Make the necessary Adjustments. Then, in the words of Winston Churchill "Never give up. Never give up. Never ever give up."

Resources

Books

Success through a Positive Mental Attitude by Napoleon Hill

How to Win Friends and Influence People by Dale Carnegie

Multiple Streams of Income and *Multiple Streams of Internet Income* by Robert Allen

System

The Photo Reading Whole Mind System by Paul Sheele

:01
One Minute Review
Parting Thoughts

1. Your attitude will affect your outcome. Guard it closely.

2. The more you know, the more you realize there is to learn. Commit yourself to lifelong learning.

3. Capital (cash) is the lifeblood of every business. Keep your eye on the cash register.

4. Add streams of income, but only after your core stream is consistent and systematized.

Congratulations! You're Ready for Your Next Step.

I'd like to help you get started NOW so I'm offering you

a FREE, no obligation 30 minute

Zero to Success Strategy session

with one of my specially trained business strategists.

During this powerful session you will:

- ◑ Uncover your unique talents and experience that you can use to help you launch a successful business.

- ◑ Learn how to overcome the fear and uncertainty that's been holding you back.

- ◑ Decide on an action plan that will move you toward your dreams.

Let's Get Started Now.
Just call us at 888-695-2765 or send me an email to
Drew@zerotosuccess.com.

Again, Congratulations! You're on your way to success.

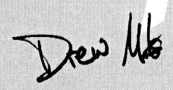

Wouldn't it be great to have a trusted guide or mentor who could hold your hand and guide you through the 'Tough Stuff'—literally tell you what you need to do and know in order to succeed in your own business?

Starting and growing a company is like taking a trip, if you do your research before you set out you'll be mindful of the detours, roadblocks and possible traffic jams; while taking a trip without proper planning can leave you disabled on the side of the road. Of course, even the best planned routes can lead down unexpected paths

Zero 2 Success Coaching Will Show You:

- ↺ **What it takes to build—and protect—wealth.**
- ↺ **Why having a business of your own is job #1.**
- ↺ **Why working with coaches and mentors doesn't really cost you money since it can save you years of trial and error and untold thousands of dollars.**
- ↺ **The nuts and bolts of business success.**
- ↺ **The benefits and pitfalls of partnering with others.**
- ↺ **How to spread the word about your business.**
- ↺ **The real truth about business plans and why you need one.**

In our "Zero to Success" business mentoring program you will work one on one with a highly trained business coach who will help guide you down the road to Success.

If you're finally ready to get off the fence and start your own business —OR, even if you already have a business, but it's not living up to its financial potential—"Zero to Success" business coaching is *exactly* what you need.

Wealth Building Programs From Pathfinder Business Strategies

Wealth Builder's University is packed end-to-end with proven, results-driven content rich in information and carefully designed to make you succeed. This monthly program consists of TWO audio CDs, newsletter, and transcription delivered to your door. This is more than a source of knowledge; it's an experience of wealth creation that will have a permanent impact on your life. Here's just a little of what you will learn: How to turn goals into action and actions into wealth; How to master YOUR money; and how to get out of debt and stay out. It's what they didn't teach you in school, brought to your home or office every month.

Incorporating Brilliance you will learn the "How To's" of maximizing the advantages from your corporation. This program consists of over 5 hours of audio instruction and an all inclusive workbook. Through this system you will learn how to: Maximize the 300 deductions that are available to businesses; Avoid the self-employment "penalty" tax; Protect your personal assets from judgments and liens; Dust off your existing corporation and start using it to your advantage. This is the program that made Drew Miles reputation as "The Wealth Building Attorney".

Wealth Accumulation System contains real-world techniques and strategies to make you financially sound and secure. The program consists of two information packed CDs and two bonus reports. You can make all the money your heart desires in real estate, the internet, information marketing or anything else, but if you are not properly protected it can blow up in your face. That's why you *must* have this program. This is a systematic approach to keeping more of your hard earned money and parleying it into a lifetime of success and happiness. This is required information for anyone concerned about their future.

BONUS

Enhancing Lives Through Quality
Financial Education

SIGN UP TODAY
FOR YOUR SUBSCRIPTION TO
WEALTH BUILDER'S UNIVERSITY
2 MONTHS FREE!
A $59.97 VALUE

WEALTH BUILDER'S UNIVERSITY

It's the monthly wealth building financial newsletter from Drew Miles and Pathfinder Business Strategies LLC that's packed with results-driven content and tax-saving tips designed to make you succeed in business and in life.

Each month you get 2 audio CD's, an information packed newsletter and a full transcription delivered to your door.

<u>Act now!</u> Send in this coupon today and start getting Wealth Builder's University delivered to your door... FREE! After the first two months you can continue to receive Wealth Builders University and we will charge your credit card $29.95 per month*. You can cancel your subscription at any time.

Here's just some of what you will learn:

Turning Goals Into Action; Mastering Your Money; Getting Out Of Debt and Staying That Way!

This is the one University that teaches you what you didn't learn in school. Don't waste another moment in the financial dark. Subscribe to Wealth Builder's University and begin to see the light!

Mail in the coupon below or
go to **www.pfbs.com/wealthbuilders** and get started!

Yes Drew! Send me 2 months of Wealth Builder's University <u>FREE!</u>

Name: _____

Address: _____

Email: _____ Telephone: _____

Credit Card type: _____ Credit Card #: _____ Exp: _____

Mail this coupon to:
Pathfinder Business Strategies LLC
10315 102nd Terrace
Sebastian, FL 32958

---

*Shipping and handling not included.

Printed in the United States
58774LVS00004B/1-120